Dear Abby,

You are a wonderful person, a good friend and it's a pleasure having you here in Seattle.

I hope you enjoy this book and your future includes many "Computers for profit."

Your new friend,

David Lyghster

COMPUTERS
FOR PROFIT

COMPUTERS FOR PROFIT

Understanding, Evaluating,
Selecting, and Implementing
Computer Systems

DAVID C.
DYKSTRA

RESTON PUBLISHING COMPANY, INC.

 A Prentice-Hall Company

Reston, Virginia

Library of Congress Cataloging in Publication Data

Dykstra, David C.
    Computers for profit.

    Includes index.
    1. Electronic digital computers—Purchasing.
2. Business—Data processing. I. Title.
HF5548.2.D94 1983   001.64′068′7   83–4413
ISBN 0–8359–0868–2
ISBN 0–8359–0867–4 (pbk.)

*Editorial/production supervision and
interior design by* NORMA M. KARLIN

© 1983 by Reston Publishing Company, Inc.
A Prentice-Hall Company
Reston, Virginia 22090

10 9 8 7 6 5 4 3 2

PRINTED IN THE UNITED STATES OF AMERICA

To my wife, Ello

CONTENTS

PREFACE

Computers for Profit is a must for everyone who is, or potentially will be, dealing with computers in a business environment. This book is written in plain, nontechnical English.

The computerized "office of the future" is upon us. All office workers will be working with computers and computer information. It is not important for most users and managers to know how the computer works, but it is important to know how to acquire and utilize profitably the right computerized productivity tools.

The information and tools provided in this book will enable you to meet the challenges and opportunities presented by the computerized world with confidence and without fear. You will know when and how to use successfully the powerful computer tool in your business. You will know how to determine what products to buy and whom to buy them from. You will be able to make a computer pay for itself in less than one year.

The most common factor causing fear in the purchase and implementation of new computer systems is the unknown. The second most common factor is the perceived danger or risk. In fact, the perceived dangers and risks of acquiring or using a computer are real, as evidenced by the many horror stories in the computer industry. In this book we will also discuss many of the dangers and risks relating to computers. We cannot ignore the potential problems and pretend they do not exist. Understanding the dangers, however, will allow the potential user to overcome the fear of the unknown and become properly prepared for the acquisition and use of a powerful, exciting tool.

It is as dangerous to expose a business's management procedures and records to a misdirected or poorly piloted computer as it is to travel on an untested jet airplane with an inexperienced pilot. Millions of people, however, do fly each year, having assured themselves, on the basis of the track record of the airlines, that flying is safe. Most airline passengers do not or need to understand the details of how airplanes work. They fly without fear because they understand the *basic principles* of how a plane flies and because they have a basic understanding of the airline industry, its companies, and the related services and quality control.

Most business professionals and managers do not want to be involved with the details or the piloting of the computer. They just want to use the computer as a tool to get them where they want to go. They need the assistance of computer professionals, who may be sales personnel, their own in-house staff, or independent consultants. Unfortunately, because of the rapid growth in the computer industry, there are many poorly qualified people claiming to be experts or professionals. Many businesses have or use experts with the wrong specialty expertise.

A computer is a service productivity tool for a business. Buying a computer, therefore, means buying an ongoing service rather than a hard and fixed asset. This service will come from the computer itself but, more importantly, from the professionals who support the computer installation. The information contained in this book will enable the noncomputer experts to communicate with and understand the computer experts. Any reader of this book will be able to identify and properly use the best computer advisors, salespeople, sales organizations, and products for their needs. They will know that their computers and their pilots are safe to fly.

Each chapter of this book is designed to stand alone, the reader being easily able to reference the topic of interest. Readers can reference materials and information presented as their computer maturity progresses or as they grow from thinking, understanding, looking and buying, to implementing and improving a computer system.

Operators, office supervisors, and managers will find that this book contains the necessary information for them to survive and succeed in the computerized world. This applies to independent business organizations looking for their first computer up to the managers and professionals in large organizations who need to better utilize their computer departments, or, in many cases, make end runs around the computer departments. Business students will find this valuable for preparing for the real world.

Students and computer professionals with a technical understanding of computers will also find this book must reading. The technical details, which they already know and which are contained in numerous books, have been deliberately omitted from this book. The book, however, contains the necessary information to help the computer professional, through a better understanding of the user environment, bridge the communication gap with the noncomputer professional.

Investors and other industry observers will also find this book invaluable. The book contains a unique analysis in Chapters 6 and 7 of the computer manufacturing and sales industries. Actual statistical information relates to specific recent time periods but illustrates market conditions and the trends and conclusions based upon them. Most of the industry giants will not grow as fast as the industry. Many new companies will continue to arise, and the number of their products and services will increase. The smaller companies that specialize, provide quality and service, and are closely attuned to their professional and small business customers will be the most successful.

COMPUTERS
FOR PROFIT

UNDERSTANDING COMPUTERS AND THE COMPUTER INDUSTRY

PART ONE

1

INTRODUCTION

Computers are now so powerful and inexpensive that most businesses must use them to stay competitive. The rapid growth of the computer industry has also created a proliferation of products and salespeople. These salespeople are touting their products and services, making claims, calling their competitors' products inferior or obsolete, and promising you everything in a language most users do not understand. Most business managers end up confused and then do nothing or buy the wrong thing.

It is easy to sell a modern computer system that is better than whatever a business had or did not have before. Many businesses buy a system and are happy in their ignorance of not knowing they paid too much, got too little, or received products technologically obsolete. A large number of businesses have purchased computers that did not live up to expectations and the seller's promise. Horror stories are commonplace.

Selecting the right business computer system is an extremely important and complex task. If you decide to remove or replace a system after it is installed, it could cost you more than the system itself. For example, if you purchase a $35,000 system and decide to replace it, one year after installation, with a better $30,000 system, it could cost you $35,000 to take the old system out and convert your records to the new system, plus $30,000 for the new system. You will then have $100,000 invested in a $30,000 system. If you go back to where you were B.C. (before computer), you may have spent $70,000 for a learning experience.

It is difficult and expensive to replace a computer system, because a large amount of the business' critical records become filed within the system. The main benefit of a computerized business information system is efficient and accurate record storage with rapid information retrieval, analysis, and reporting. When a system needs to be replaced, it is generally because the records are in disarray and the system is poorly documented.

Many first-time purchasers of a business computer spend 25 to 50 percent more than they need to spend, receive an inadequate system, and/or spend an additional 50 to 100 percent correcting the deficiencies of the original purchase. Many businesses with computer systems are not satisfied with their systems but are not changing, due to the high conversion costs. Furthermore, similar businesses with similar systems have a cost range of over 2.5 to 1 for what they have paid for their systems, and there does not appear to be any correlation between cost and satisfaction. A $40,000 system may be working as well as a $100,000 system.

Some of the more expensive systems are overly complex, generate too much paper and information, and are difficult to modify. Some inexpensive systems are slow, lack adequate training, documentation and vendor support, and are easily outgrown due to either business growth or new applications requirements.

Thousands of computer systems are available to businesses. New systems are being developed to cover deficiencies of existing systems, to incorporate the latest technology, or to better handle a unique situation. Each business is unique: what is best for one business may not work for another business.

A recent survey indicated that over 75 percent of first-time computer system purchasers are not completely satisfied with their systems. The unsatisfactory results were usually not primarily the fault of the original system or vendor, but the purchasers' not understanding their own requirements in relation to the systems' capabilities.

COMPUTER CONCEPTS AND TERMS

The first step for a successful computer system purchase is education. You must know what you are getting into. You do not need to be an expert, but you must understand the "experts." You must understand the hardware and software products and how they function.

The business user and purchaser should avoid getting bogged down in technical details. Being overly involved in the details of how a computer works can hinder the management and use of a computer.

Buying a computer or computer service is a lot like buying or leasing a car. You don't really care about all the details on how it works; you just want it to get you where you are going dependably. In fact, you don't want to think or worry about what is going on inside the engine.

Many mistakes are made because the user or purchaser is intimidated by the apparent knowledge and jargon of the computer seller. Many sellers use the intimidation position and the purchaser's fear to sell the most profitable system but, many times, the wrong system for the purchaser. Many weak salespeople with inferior products use fancy jargon as a means to cover up their weaknesses.

Chapters 2 through 7 review and explain the basic terms, concepts, products, sources, and the industry. The understanding obtained will place the user and manager on an even level with the technical and sales "experts." With this knowledge, you will be surprised to find that many so-called experts are poorly informed and out of date. You will quickly gain the knowledge and confidence necessary to properly deal with the computer professionals and to identify the nonprofessionals.

USER REQUIREMENTS

An effective computer system requires a change in the method of processing, filing, analyzing, and reporting information and the management of these activities. You must understand how these activities will be performed in the computer environment. You must be able to compare and evaluate vendors' proposals.

The most important ingredient of a successful system purchase is customer-prepared requirements and specifications. You must know what you want now and in the future. You must specify what records are going to be filed, for how long, and how they are going to be cross-referenced, analyzed, summarized, and reported.

Requirement and specification preparation requires an understanding of the personal styles involved within the business (and later of the vendor), all aspects of the business, information priorities, file management, and features and capabilities of a computerized record management, analysis, and reporting system. The requirements and specifications must be clearly documented.

When you decide to contract for a business computer system, a complete software and hardware system should be specified. This means that all major, basic systems that are interrelated should be included. Minor changes and new applications will generally be added later, but the initial system should include all interrelated applications and activities.

Chapters 8 through 11 provide you the necessary tools to identify and justify when and how to use a computer for profit and how to prepare your requirements. You will be able to identify which areas should be computerized and document your requirements so you get what you need.

VENDOR EVALUATION AND SELECTION

The vendors generally have the largest profit margin in the hardware. Therefore, you have the greatest leverage when you negotiate for a complete software system with the hardware. Some vendors try to sell hardware with a partial software system with the idea to "try a little computerization to start, and we'll add the rest later." The rest is usually added with great difficulty, and many times the hardware (which has now been purchased or leased) is not adequate.

The most important ingredients in selecting a vendor are, in order: (1) the individuals with whom you will be working; (2) the software; and (3) the hardware brand. The people are most important because they must be able to tailor the system to fit the personality and requirements of your business. Do not buy a Brooks Brothers suit and have your butcher do the alterations.

Many vendors should be evaluated. Reference checks must

be thorough and should include on-site visits at installations that are similar to yours.

When you sign a contract, make sure you understand it. Make sure that the hardware and software products are specified and that payments prior to delivery and proof of performance are minimized.

Chapter 12 and Appendix 2 provide specific brand features and criteria for evaluating vendors.

INSTALLATION AND IMPLEMENTATION

Implementing a computer system is never as easy as the purchaser expects it to be. Manual systems or old-style computer systems required many redundant steps to assure control. Current computers are so powerful that old style controls and procedures are no longer necessary. They can be replaced with descriptive and summary information which is easier to input and use.

The final design, testing, and implementation specifications and procedures are critical factors for success. It will take considerable time and effort to establish coding systems and then code and load the data into the computer system. Security procedures are a major concern for a computer installation.

Chapter 13 covers the key techniques required for a successful computer implementation or conversion and easy ongoing operation. Topics covered are the contract, progress payments and milestones, human factors, training, and security.

CONFLICTING ADVISORS

When a business is considering a computer or a change in an existing system, the business will hear a great deal of conflicting advice. Consultants will tell you, "Don't trust the salesman," and the salesman will tell you, "Don't trust the consultants." The members of each group are like economists in that they cannot agree on much among themselves.

When it comes to advice on business computers, the best advice is "Don't trust anyone." Use the business common sense that has got you where you are—and be careful. Question and analyze all the advice you receive.

Chapter 14 discusses which computer professionals and advisors are best in which situations. You will be provided the tools to evaluate consultants and other advisors. Many times a good sales organization, along with proper user effort and knowledge, will make use of a third-party consultant unnecessary. Good consultants can be extremely valuable in many situations.

SOURCES OF INFORMATION ON BUSINESS COMPUTERS

I have read or reviewed hundreds of books on business computers and found most are unsatisfactory. They are generally written by someone who has a background with large business systems and/ or has never worked producing real goods or services. Many of the concepts and practices they recommend are not practical or cost effective in relation to the current availability of low-cost packaged or easily customized software/hardware systems. Current, nontechnical periodicals seem to be the best source, but many articles should be treated with skepticism for the same reasons noted above.

The contents of this book have digested key features from many books, articles, and sources. This information will enable you to analyze and extract information from articles you will read in the future. You will be able to judge the quality of information of an article and tell whether it is coming from someone who knows, someone in a theory-laden ivory tower, a general writer filling copy space, or an advertiser's influence.

DON'T EXPECT TOO MUCH

One of the biggest dangers in buying a business computer system is for the business to expect too much. Many salesmen or consultants will recommend too sophisticated and complex a system and promise all kinds of fantastic things it will do, like make all your decisions for you. The role of the first computer you buy is not to make your decisions, but to process the basic information and give you timely and accurate reports covering the interrelated activities within your business—so *you* can make better decisions. Also, remember that the computer is very stupid, so it is going to take time and effort to get a properly working computer system.

For most businesses, a true business computer that provides management information will require some customized software. A computer with only prepackaged accounting software is just an electronic bookkeeping machine and has been a gross disappointment to most purchasers. If you want a true business computer system, you must know what you want it to do, specify that, and *buy the software before the hardware.*

POTENTIAL IS GREATER THAN PROBLEMS

The potential problems involved should not discourage you from making a valuable, cost-effective computer system acquisition. A computer can do many things fast and accurately. It follows directions. It is not mentally distracted. It can do these things better than people and at less than one-tenth to as little as one-hundredth (depending on the application) the cost of people.

Computers generally do not replace people, but enable people to put their efforts to productive, creative activities that the computer cannot perform. Business productivity and profitability often substantially increase with a proper people/computer combination.

Computers for Profit is a no-nonsense explanation of how to use profitably modern electronic computer power in business management. The book provides advice and answers to many problems facing a business manager and computer user. It explains, in nontechnical language, what you need to know to properly purchase, manage, and utilize today's powerful electronic computers.

2

UNDERSTANDING COMPUTERS—I

It is not necessary for a computer user or purchaser to understand the details of how a system works. It is not necessary to understand anything if the computer does exactly what the purchaser wants and the requirements will never change. You could buy a $10 calculator or electronic game (computer) just as you would buy a radio.

If you are buying a computer system for management information, you probably cannot get all your requirements from a box ordered and delivered like a refrigerator. Furthermore, your requirements will probably change in the future. In this case you must understand some of the basic concepts and complexities of how a computer works. You need to be able to specify what you want and manage the initial purchase and future changes.

Many times, computers are not properly controlled and directed (managed) because managers and users do not understand the computer, its salespeople, and its programmers. The computer user or business manager is often dazzled with a multitude of terms by programmers and salespeople, which creates a communication barrier.

Every discipline has its language and terms that are necessary for understanding it. The computer field is no exception. Unfortunately, however, most glossaries are overpowering and too technical for the general business manager and user.

A manager does not need to understand the details of every activity managed. In fact, getting bogged down in details can be a hindrance to effective management. A manager must, however, have an overview type of understanding, know how to communicate with the specialists, know what results to expect, and know how to evaluate performance.

Computers are not really hard to understand from a management or user viewpoint. They are fast and stupid. That is all. You can think of a computer as 100 stupid slaves. These slaves can accurately and quickly file information, retrieve, sort, interrelate, make calculations, and summarize. They also have a very fast eraser. They remember and follow directions exactly. The one thing they cannot do is think. However, they don't daydream, take coffee breaks or vacations, gossip, or quit without notice. They are also very hard and expensive to fire.

The definitions below explain how the conceptual multitude of slaves in a computer system works. Some of them are not technically "pure," but rather, reflect their general use in management or user communication. These key concepts and terms are basically all you should need for effective general management, decision making, and computer use.

The definitions and explanations are arranged to explain how a business computer system works, starting with the equipment and proceeding through the printed results. Many terms are defined shortly after they are introduced. In computer systems, the final output is what is most important. Therefore, it may be helpful, in order to have a clear understanding of a business computer system, to read the list of definitions as presented and then read it by paragraph in reverse order. You should then review the alphabetical listing and briefer descriptions of these key terms in Appendix 1, "Glossary."

Figure 2–1 illustrates some of the components of a working computer system. Table 2–1 lists standard computer term conversion factors.

Computer System

Computer (*CPU*); *Mass Storage* device(s); *CRT*(s) or *VDT*(s); *Printer*(s); and *Software*.

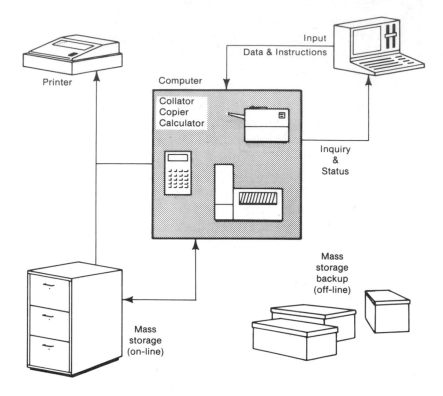

FIGURE 2–1 How a Computer System Works: Hardware Devices

CPU, Computer

*C*entral *P*rocessing *U*nit. *Computer.* The brains. Does the computing and gives directions. Receives information files, retrieves, erases, revises, calculates, summarizes, and gives directions to other units in the system. Box of electronic chips and circuits. In a microcomputer the CPU is a single chip. There is no clear distinction between microcomputers, minicomputers, and mainframe computers. Figures 2–2 through 2–4 show some typical CPU boards.

Micro

*Micro*computers range in price from about $1,000 to $50,000 and are common in small businesses. Less expensive micros are

Table 2–1
COMPUTER CONVERSION FACTORS

Bit	Binary digit; 0 or 1.
Byte	8 bits, or one character (0,1,2, . . . ,9 or A,B,C, . . . ,Z).
K	Kilo; 1,000 characters or bytes; $\frac{1}{3}$ page (single-spaced typed).
64K	Common CPU memory size; 20 pages, or one Manila file.
M	Mega, million.
MB	Million bytes or characters; 300 pages, 15 Manila files, or one 3-inch Redrope file pocket.
10MB	3,000 pages, 10 books, or one standard file drawer.
40MB	One four-drawer file cabinet.
cps	characters per second; one cps equals twelve 5-character words per minute.
lpm	lines per minute; (for 8½-inch paper at 60 typed characters average per line, one lpm = one cps).
60cps	one page per minute, or 720 5-character words per minute.

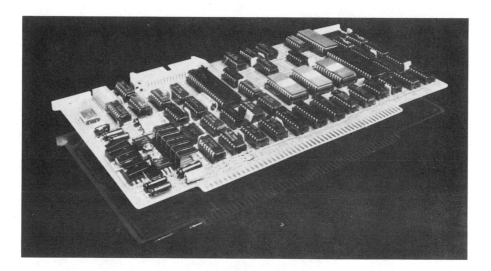

FIGURE 2–2 CPU and Memory Board

FIGURE 2–3 Computer and Memory Boards for a Multiprocessor Microcomputer

FIGURE 2–4 Connecting or "Mother" Board for a Multiboard Microcomputer

single-user (personal) systems. The expensive micros have more computers within the computer that permit multiple users to simultaneously use the computer. Figures 2–5 and 2–6 show a typical microcomputer.

FIGURE 2–5 (Top) Microcomputer with Integrated Floppy Disk Drive; (Bottom) Floppy Disk Drive Expansion Unit for Above Computer

FIGURE 2–6 Inside of Previous Computer

Mini

*Mini*computers range in price from $20,000 to $1 million and are the most common general business types. Minis generally have a more complex design than micros that permits more users and more sophisticated applications.

Mainframe

Mainframe computers are the large $500,000 to multimillion-dollar-priced computers. Mainframes can handle very large volumes of data for many users at many locations.

Personal, Desk-top

Personal or *desk-top* computers are so named because they are compact and fit in a small space, such as on a desk top. The terminal and CPU are usually one unit. The printer is adjacent and requires little space. They are "personal" because they do only one thing at one time for one person. They operate independently of a larger computer and other users. They may, however, communicate with other computers. Figure 2–7 shows a desk-top computer system.

CPU Memory, Bytes, K

CPU capacity is expressed in bytes or characters (A, B, C, . . . 1, 2, 3, . . . , etc.) of information and instructions stored and available for processing at any one time. This CPU capacity is called the "memory" of the computer and is usually expressed in thousand or "K" (like kilo) units, such as 64K; 64K is about 22 single-spaced typed pages. CPU memory is lost when power is lost or turned off.

FIGURE 2–7 Desk-top Computer System

Virtual Memory

Virtual memory is where memory data are temporarily filed and retrieved from mass storage to RAM so quickly, that the user is not aware that it is happening. This process increases effective memory capacity.

RAM

Random Access Memory is a desired feature because it more efficiently utilizes the available space. It is the working memory for the CPU. RAM information is randomly filed and accessed as required by the CPU for the project being performed.

Bit

A *bit* signifies an on-off electrical or magnetic charge.

Word Size, Bytes

The *word size,* or length, determines the number of bits the computer can understand in a single image. An increase in word size increases the vocabulary, speed, and capability of the computer. Eight-bit words (a byte) are required for all character definitions and minimum understanding of instructions. Sixteen-bit words (4 times or more the capability of 8-bit words) are most common in business minicomputers. Thirty-two-bit words (16 times or more the capability of 8-bit words) are common in scientific/engineering minicomputers where complex calculations are required.

Mass Storage (MB)

The "file cabinets." Capacity is expressed in million (mega) bytes (characters) or MB; 1.0 MB equals about 350 single-spaced typed pages. Data are stored with charges that are not altered when power is off. This is the permanent "memory"; however, it can be easily erased and revised. The common magnetic mass storage media are floppy disks (diskettes), hard disks, and tape. Bubble memory is the newest medium.

Record

Record is a term used to denote stored information pertaining to a certain item, e.g., *customer record.*

File

All the records of a certain type. For example, all the customer records make up the *customer file.*

Variable-Length Records

A desirable mass storage feature without which storage space would have to be kept available for all possible information. Variable-length records use space only as required for actual data.

Disk

Disks work like phonograph records. However, the read (play), erase, and write (record) functions work more like a tape recorder/player. A disk spins rapidly, and the reading and writing heads (like phonograph needles) move rapidly back and forth or are fixed in contact with all magnetic channels (like grooves), giving rapid random access filing, retrieving, and updating capability.

Floppy Disks, Diskettes

Small 3- to 8-inch flexible, removable disks in protective paper sleeves. Capacity ranges from 80K on a $5^1/_4$-inch single side (about 27 single-spaced typed pages) to 1.2 MB (400 pages) on an 8-inch double-density, double-side diskette. Can be used for on-line processing or backup. Not as fast or as reliable as hard disks, but advantages are low cost, flexibility, and ease of backup. Floppy diskettes are shown in Fig. 2–8.

FIGURE 2-8 Floppy Diskettes—5¼ inch and 8 inch

Hard Disks

Hard platters that are removable via a cartridge medium or fixed within a cabinet. Capacity varies from 2 MB on a disk to 200 MB (two hundred 350-page books) on a multiplatter cartridge. Reliability and speed are very good with hard disks. Backup data can be stored on removable cartridges; however, they are often stored on lower cost floppy disks or magnetic tape.

Winchester

Winchester is the code name for the most common high-technology, hermetically sealed, fixed hard-disk units. Figure 2-9 shows a Winchester hard-disk subsystem and controller board.

FIGURE 2–9 Hard-disk Subsystem and Controller Board

Disk Drive

The device that reads the data on a disk or diskette and transmits the information to the computer. The drive also responds to commands from the computer to file, erase, and re-sort information on the disk or diskette.

Magnetic Tape

Cassettes or reel-to-reel. Used primarily for backup. Not usually used for on-line processing because they do not have the advantage of rapid random access that disks have.

Bubble Memory

Electronic chips within the CPU that do not lose their charges or memory when power is lost. Much faster than other power-loss-insensitive media (disks or tape), but not yet cost effective for large amounts of data storage and processing. Figure 2–10 shows a bubble memory board by itself and inside a computer.

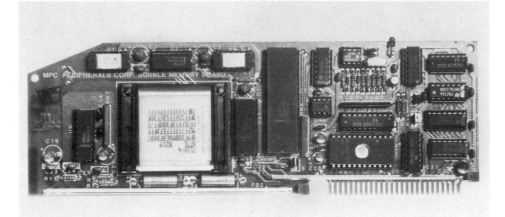

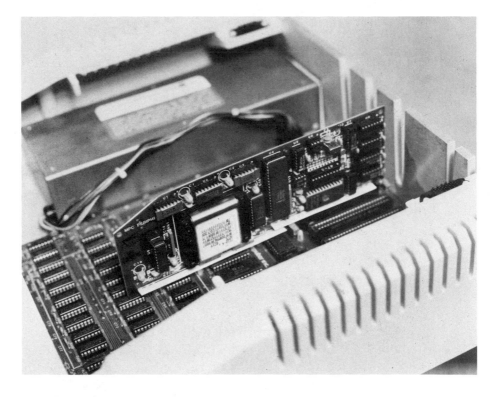

FIGURE 2–10 (Top) Bubble Memory Board; (Bottom) Above-Board, Inside Desk-top Computer

Input

Data, information, and instructions. Nearly always entered into the computer via a CRT or VDT. Keypunching and reading of cards or paper tape are obsolete for most uses.

CRT, VDT, Terminals

Cathode Ray Tubes or *Video Display Tubes* (*Terminals*) are used for input and inquiry. They consist of a TV screen and a keyboard with typewriter, adding machine, and special instruction keys. Some units contain limited memory (their own CPU) to facilitate input via "intelligent" prompting and editing. A terminal is shown in Fig. 2–11.

Punched Cards

Obsolete cardboard cards used for data. A data storage medium that has been replaced by disks and tape.

Paper Tape

Obsolete narrow rolls of paper used for data. A data storage medium that has been replaced by disks and tape.

Output

Information received by the user from the computer.

Hard Copy

Reports (output) printed on paper.

Soft Copy

Information (output) received on the CRT screen without printing. Usually requested for selected items or items in a requested category or range.

FIGURE 2–11 Cathode Ray Tube (CRT) or Video Display Tube (VDT) Terminal

Printers

The four main types of printers are line character, letter quality, dot-matrix line and dot-matrix character.

Spooling

Printers print much slower than a computer works. A computer can "spool" or store data in a designated mass storage location. The printer retrieves data from this location at its speed while the computer does something else at its speed.

Line Printers (lpm)

Line printers print an entire line at one time, and speeds are usually expressed in *lines per minute*, or *lpm*. The most common speeds are 300 lpm and 600 lpm. A 300 lpm printer can generate over 50,000 pages per month, or more than ten managers who like to read a lot can use.

Band, Chain

Band, or chain, line printer characters are solid, generally with capital letters, normal signs, and numbers.

Character Printers (cps)

Character printers print a character at a time, and speeds are expressed in *characters per second*, or *cps;* 55 cps, a common speed, equals 660 words per minute, or ten times the speed of a good typist. One cps is about equal to one lpm, but can be faster when lines are skipped or there is little data per line.

Daisywheel, Thimble, Selectric

Letter-quality character printers have typewriter quality, print upper and lower case, and have changeable type styles. A daisywheel printer has a small wheel that has spokes with the letters at the end on small plates. Thimble printers are similar, except the spokes and plates are in a thimble configuration. A Selectric, or ball, type printer looks like a Selectric typewriter; these are not often used in a computer system due to adverse high speed and usage effects on the numerous mechanical parts. A sample of letter-quality printing is shown in Fig. 2–12. Figure 2–13 shows a daisywheel.

Dot Matrix

Dot matrix printers form characters by using small dots in a matrix format. These can be either "line" or "character" printers. These printers are usually lower priced than solid character printers for the same speed. Speed can be expressed in cps or lpm. Features may include varying larger or smaller characters for titles or compressed reports. A dot matrix printer is shown in Fig. 2–14 (p. 28), and a sample of its printouts is shown in Figs. 2–15 and 2–16 (pp. 29 and 30).

Hardware

All of the above computer equipment and devices.

Some of the features with word processing and daisywheel or thimble printing include left and right margin justification, proportional spacing, **bold** and **very bold** type. True proportional spacing is like typesetting where mmm's, www's and CAPITAL LETTERS take more space than iiiiiiiiiiiiii's and llllllllllllll's.

These features can be important for that professional look.

Other available print styles will enable you to customize your forms and documents. Available print styles include:

Regular **ten pitch** letters like this,

or **fifteen pitch** compressed print which is useful for **large documents, notes** to contracts, or **instructions** on a form. Note how you can have indented paragraphs with indented left and right margin justification.

FIGURE 2–12 Reproduction of Letter-Quality Printout (Actual Size)

FIGURE 2–13 Daisywheel for Letter-Quality Printer

Peripherals

CRTs (or VDTs), printers, and mass storage devices are peripherals. Peripherals are all the hardware except the box housing the CPU and related chips. Peripherals almost always cost more than the CPU.

I/Os

Input/Output devices. All peripherals except mass storage are I/Os. An I/O controller board for six peripherals is shown as Fig. 2–17.

Program

A set of instructions. The computer will do exactly what it is told to do. It will precisely interpret information based on prior

FIGURE 2–14 Dot Matrix Printer

instructions, becoming "programmed." It cannot think. Input signals cause the electronics to behave in such manner that subsequent input signals will be stored and interpreted in a desired manner.

Software

Programs input into the computer that make the computer do what you want it to do.

Firmware

Instructions (programs) permanently imbedded in CPU electronic devices by the manufacturer. Usually operating system type instructions. Firmware is also used in computers designed

```
STANDARD  FEATURES  INCLUDE:
```

* MICROPROCESSOR CONTROL
* 180 CPS PRINT SPEED
* BIDIRECTIONAL/LOGIC SEEKING
* 2000 CHARACTER BUFFER
* 9X7 DOT MATRIX
* EXPANDED CHARACTERS
* ADJUSTABLE PRINTHEAD/ 1-6 COPIES
* 96 ASCII CHARACTER SET
* CARTRIDGE RIBBON
* 132 COLUMN PRINT WIDTH (217 @ 16.5 CPI)
* TRACTOR FEED (FRONT OR BOTTOM)
* SELF-TEST
* X-ON/X-OFF AND DTR HANDSHAKING
* TERMINAL STATUS INDICATORS
* PAPER-OUT DETECTION

THIS IS THE FULL 128 ASCII CHARACTER SET (TRANSPARENCY

!"#$%&'()*+,-./0123456789:;<=>?@A

FIGURE 2-15 Reproduction of Dot Matrix Printout (Actual Size)

for single dedicated purposes, such as calculators, production control, stereo equipment, or electronic games.

Application Software

Instructions (programs) that tell the computer how to receive and process information received that pertains to a particular application.

Operating System (OS) and Compiler

The initial instructions, software, and/or firmware provided by the manufacturer that enables the computer to understand

DATASOUTH'S DS-180 MATRIX PRINTER

INTRODUCTION TO THE DS-180 MATRIX PRINTER

The Datasouth DS-180 is a serial matrix printer capable of producing highly
legible copy on forms containing as many as six parts. It is well suited
to a variety of applications ranging from a CRT slave printer to small business
systems. The standard ASCII code is employed, and communications may
be performed over a serial interface at BAUD rates ranging from 110 to 9600.
A TTL parallel interface is also standard and is compatible with the CENTRONICS
convention.

THE GRAPHICS CAPABILITY OF THE DS-180 WILL GENERATE:

BARCODES

GRAPHS

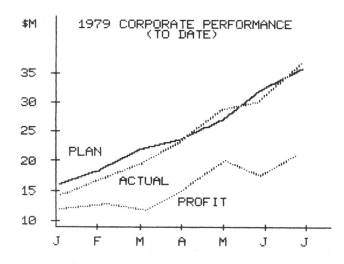

Figure 2–16 Reproduction of Dot Matrix Printout (Reduced Size)

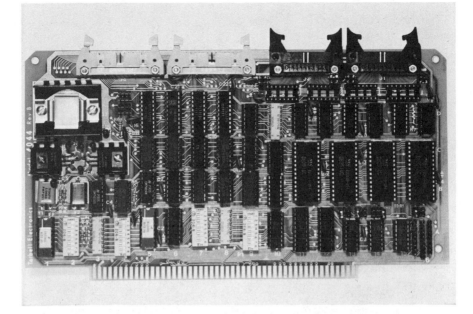

FIGURE 2–17 I/O Controller Board with 6 Ports

instruction words. The base dictionary of the system. Includes communication, filing, and processing features.

Language

The vocabulary, defined by the compiler, that enables the computer to understand application software.

BASIC, COBOL, FORTRAN, PASCAL, RPG

Common languages for application programs. Certain operating systems and languages are best for certain purposes. The languages (compilers) are usually supplied by the CPU manufacturer. A language with the same name may not work on another manufacturer's CPU.

Word Processing

An application program for processing words. Usually provides for easy text editing and correcting, moving paragraphs and phrases, automatic line and page adjustment, automatic addressing of letters with information from another file, etc. A word processing system is shown in Fig. 2–18. A CRT screen with word processing commands is shown in Fig. 2–19.

FIGURE 2–18 Letter-Quality Printer and Terminal Being Used for Word Processing

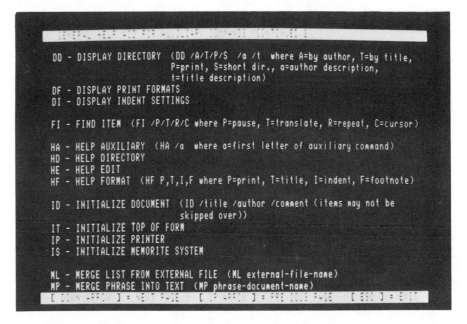

FIGURE 2–19 CRT Screen with Word Processing Commands

Data Base (or File) Management System (DBMS)

An intermediate program for an English-type language application program that, in relatively few instructions, will create special reports from data in the files.

Turnkey System

A computer system that is fully operational when, after it is delivered and installed, the user merely "turns the key." The system includes application software that has been tested with the user's data prior to delivery.

RFP

Request For Proposal from a computer vendor, usually to provide a turnkey system to meet user requirements.

GIGO

Garbage *In*, Garbage *Out*. A common expression meaning that bad input or programs will give bad results.

KISS

Keep It Simple, *Stupid.* A common expression advising that computer systems design ought to be kept simple.

3

UNDERSTANDING COMPUTERS—II

It is obvious that the capacities and speeds of a computer system are enormous. It's easy for a computer system to bury an organization in data and paper. Operating security and control are vulnerable.

There are numerous variables that go into the makeup of a computer system and its components. Features, capability, quality, and price will vary widely among the producers and their products. There are over 3,000 companies that produce the end-user computer system components.

Application software has the greatest variation. It is also the major factor in determining the hardware, operating system, and language requirements. Many businesses spend more than ten times what they need to spend for software. Many users spend four times as much for software as for hardware despite the fact that the software should cost much less than the hardware.

The peripherals have the next greatest variation. They are the next most important factor in determining the CPU and operating system requirements. Many leading name brands of computers will not accept other brand peripherals, and the name-brand peripherals may cost much more and/or may not have the proper features or may have unnecessary features for many applications.

The terms and concepts of the preceding chapter should be sufficient for most general business uses. When salespeople, consultants, or programmers try to overwhelm you with jargon you do not understand, get them back to these basics. The job of your top computer managers and advisors is not to create an esoteric niche in your organization. Their job is to bridge the communication gap. Their job is to keep you informed in your language, to serve you and your organization, and to facilitate your decisions concerning their activities and the total organization performance.

In the last chapter the basic terms and computer concepts of interest to all users were presented. Working with more complex systems or being involved with the computer operation requires understanding more terms and concepts. The concepts and terms defined below may be omitted by the general management type of user.

Computers may be programmed and operated by people with no formal or advanced training. They should, however, have support from skilled, trained personnel. These terms will be sufficient for understanding state-of-the-art sophisticated computers for which additional technical support is available. They are still basic, however, to the computer professional who has a more extended computer vocabulary received from a computer science education.

As in Part I, the following concepts and terms are arranged starting with equipment and proceeding through printed results.

Digital Computer

In an electronic digital computer all logic is represented by combinations of the presence or absence of electrical charges (on or off switches). Digital computers are used for business applications. They are also now so powerful, that they can efficiently and accurately perform functions previously performed by analog computers.

Binary

Two. Binary digits consist of two states, a zero or a one, represented by the absence or presence of a charge, respectively.

Digital

Pertaining to discrete items or logic. In a digital computer all logic is performed by binary digits.

Analog Computer

A computer whose logic comes from a continuous range of power or signals. These are useful for complex mathematical applications. An analog computer can represent exact functions such as one divided by three or the square root of three. A digital computer must approximate these functions with many digits after the decimal point.

ROM

*R*ead-*O*nly *M*emory. Instructions permanently housed in memory. Firmware.

PROM

*P*rogrammable *R*ead-*O*nly *M*emory. ROM that may be altered by the user.

Core

The center of a piece of magnetic-iron-type material that was the memory of early electronic (vacuum tube) computers. Although the physical "core" no longer exists, the term is still used to refer to the main (or CPU) memory.

Chip, Wafer

An electronic device. Pure materials, usually silicon, with special electronic properties are made into pure cylinders and sliced into *wafers* about one inch in diameter or larger. These wafers are then photo-coated and etched to make many small rectangular devices the size of the head of a pin. The devices are cut from the wafer, and the individual device is the *chip*. Single devices, like transistors and others equivalent to a vacuum tube, have been made this way for many years. Entire CPUs and other complex electronic devices, the equivalent of many vacuum tubes, are now manufactured on a single chip. A computer unit consists of CPU, memory, and controller chips. A computer unit may consist of many interconnected chips on a circuit board or boards. A block diagram for a computer chip, the Intel 8080, is shown in Fig. 3–1.

Microprocessor

A CPU on a single chip.

LSI

*L*arge *S*cale *I*ntegration. The term refers to the technology of making complex electronic chips with the equivalent of thousands of devices on a single chip.

MOS

*M*etal *O*xide *S*emiconductor. The term refers to the technology used to create most LSI chips by means of layering materials on a wafer. Most CPU microprocessors are LSI MOS chips.

Controller

A *controller* is a computer within the computer system. It is the computer that "controls" the activities between devices and the operation of these devices. Disk drives, printers, and CRTs all have controllers. The design of the CPUs, ROMs (firmware), and controllers, along with that of the operating system, determines the advanced features of the computer system.

Multiuser, Multitasking, Multiprogramming

Features of a computer that permit apparently simultaneous activities. The computer switches or rotates from activities so

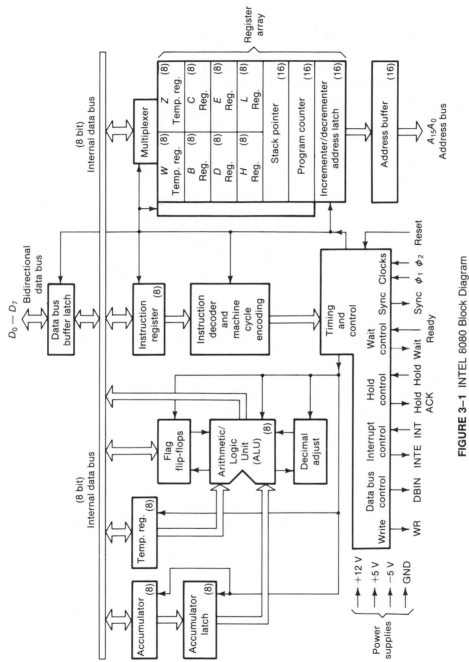

FIGURE 3–1 INTEL 8080 Block Diagram

39

rapidly, that the users do not notice that their individual jobs have been interrupted. The *multiuser* feature is for more than one user and can be for the same or different applications. *Multitasking* permits the simultaneous operation of different tasks, such as entering different types of data or entering data and printing. *Multiprogramming* permits simultaneous access to and processing with different programs.

Foreground

A task performed by the computer that prevents the CRT from being used for other input or inquiry is called the "foreground" task.

Background

A task performed by the computer in a "background" or internal mode is not apparent to the operator. The operator may be performing another function, such as input, in the foreground mode while the computer is making calculations, sorting, or printing in the background mode. Background (sometimes called "foreground/background") is a special feature not available on less expensive computers.

Distributed Data Processing

Distributed data processing is a network of computers operating independently for some functions, but communicating and transferring data when required. In more sophisticated distributed systems the communicating and data transferring are handled automatically by the computers and the computers within the computers. For example, in a network of commercial savings banks each bank may have its own computer with data on its customers. A customer may make a deposit or withdrawal at another bank; that bank's computer will automatically call the customer's home bank computer and obtain and update the necessary account information.

Communication

The transferring of information from one computer to another computer. Computers can "talk" to each other. Communication capabilities are becoming increasingly important. Communication greatly increases the efficiency and power of a computer, as it enables a computer to operate independently but, when required, obtain information from another computer. Communication can be through a direct wire or over phone lines through a modem. (See Fig. 3–2.)

Modem

*Modulator-dem*odulator. A device that converts digital signals from a computer into voice-like signals that can be trans-

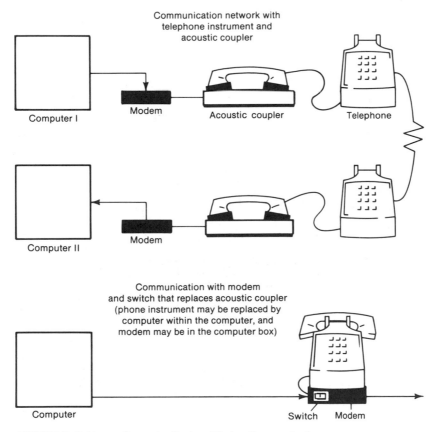

FIGURE 3–2 How a Computer System Works: Communication

mitted over a telephone line. A *modem* is required at each computer to enable two computers to "talk" to each other over a phone line. A modem with an automatic dial-up timer is shown in Fig. 3–3.

Acoustic Coupler

A device used to connect an ordinary phone to a computer system for the transferring of data. Acoustic couplers are becoming obsolete, since direct switching is now a common method. Telephone instruments are not even necessary, as the telephone instrument functions may be replaced by a computer within the computer: computers can automatically dial and answer signals over a phone line.

Baud

The rate at which data are transmitted from one computer device to another device in *bits per second;* 9600 baud is a common rate and is equivalent to 1200 characters (bytes) per second or 12,000 words per minute. A typical phone line data transmission

FIGURE 3–3 Modem with Automatic Dial-up Timer

rate is 300 baud, or 375 words per minute. The term *baud* is in honor of Baudot, a contributor to the development of computer communication.

Port

A computer connection or plug for attaching I/O and communication devices.

Bus

A circuit, communication line, or electronic path for common signals. Computers have several buses within them. There are separate buses for data, where to find the data, and how to find the data. A standard connection between devices, such as a CRT or printer and the computer, may be referred to as an RS–232 bus.

S–100

A standard internal bus for microcomputers.

RS–232

A standard I/O specification that permits modems, terminals, and printers from different manufacturers to be plugged into a computer port. *RS–232* (or RS–232C) refers to a technical specification published by the Electronics Industries Association. Sometimes called an RS–232 bus or port.

ASCII

ASCII ["ask-ee"] represents the current version of the *Amer*ican *S*tandard *C*ode for *I*nformation *I*nterchange between computers or computer devices.

Parallel

Refers to simultaneous transfer of multiple elements or blocks of data through "parallel" subcircuits. Line printers are parallel printers since a line of data is transmitted and printed at one time. The port used is called a parallel port.

Serial

Refers to the transfer of data one element or digit at a time. Character printers are sometimes called serial printers. The ports for character printers and CRTs are called serial ports.

Buffer

A chip or area on a chip for temporarily storing information. For example, if data are transmitted faster than they can be processed or printed, they are temporarily stored in a *buffer* without being lost while the second device processes the data at its own speed. A buffer is to data bits what a surge tank is to fluids.

OCR

*O*ptical *C*haracter *R*ecognition. An OCR terminal uses light and light-sensitive materials to read and transfer typewritten information into the computer.

Bar Code Reader

A fixed device or wand that uses light and light-sensitive materials to recognize standard bar codes for numbers. The device converts the numbers to digital data and transmits the data to the computer.

RJE

*R*emote *J*ob *E*ntry. An RJE device or terminal contains limited memory and can be used for accumulating data remote (disconnected) from the computer. After the data are accumulated, the device can be connected to the computer and the data transferred to the computer.

Data

Information. In a digital computer all information is in combinations of discrete bits, or binary digits, of data.

Data Processing (DP)

Synonym for *computing* or *computer.* A *data processing* device is a computer, and the data processing department or industry refers to the computer department or industry.

On-line

Data in mass storage that are accessible to the computer. The term usually refers to data on a disk or diskette that is in an operating disk drive.

Off-line

Data in mass storage that are not accessible to the computer. The data are on a tape, disk, or diskette that has been removed from the system. Backup data are off-line.

Backup

Duplicate copy of information (data) or programs not accessible to the computer. The information or programs may be stored on tape, disks, or diskettes.

Software

Descriptions of common *operating system* and *language software* for small business computers follow.

DOS

Disk Operating System. The term DOS does not refer to a standard operating system, but is used as a part of the name of a manufacturer's system. All state-of-the-art operating systems are DOSs.

CP/M

Control Program for Microcomputer. CP/M is the trademark for this operating system developed by Digital Research, Inc. This system was first installed in 1974. It is the most popular single-user operating system for personal computers.

MP/M

Multi-Programming Monitor operating system. MP/M is the trademark for this operating system developed by Digital Research, Inc. This is an enhanced version of CP/M and is the most popular multiuser operating system for microcomputers.

OASIS

An operating system developed for microcomputers by Phase One Systems, Inc. and first installed in 1977. OASIS is becoming increasingly popular and is available on many microcomputer brands. This operating system has many powerful programming and data base management system features.

UNIX and XENIX

UNIX is an operating system developed by AT & T (Bell Labs) for mini- and microcomputers. XENIX is the Microsoft (a company) version for microcomputers. UNIX and XENIX are powerful systems for time-sharing and scientific/engineering applications. They are popular with the technical community for custom programming, but there are very few business application packages available for them.

BASIC

Beginner's All-Purpose *Symbolic Instruction* Code. BASIC was developed at Dartmouth College. It is considered one of the easiest-to-learn general-purpose computer languages for business applications. It is the most commonly used language for business and personal microcomputers.

COBOL

COmmon Business Oriented Language. The most common language used for business applications on minicomputers and mainframes.

FORTRAN

FORmula TRANslator. One of the earliest developed languages. FORTRAN is used primarily for scientific- and engineering-type applications.

PASCAL

A language that has been popular for teaching, but has never been widely used for business application packages.

RPG

Report Program Generator. RPG is a common language for IBM business computers. It has never been widely accepted for other brands.

Menu

A display, on the CRT, of options that can be selected by the computer user.

Parameter

A variable element of data that can be inserted in a program or package to alter or customize the output characteristics or format.

Password

A unique sequence of characters, input as a parameter, which must again be input by the user before the computer will perform predesignated functions. Used for security and audit trails.

Package

Ready-to-use software (language or programs) sold to end users.

Electronic Spreadsheet

A software package for creating numerical data tables ("spreadsheets"). These packages facilitate the writing of application programs for financial or statistical analysis and forecasting. Computer terminals used for an electronic spreadsheet integrated with a graphics application are shown in Fig. 3–4 and 3–5.

Dealer

In the computer industry, a dealer is generally considered to be an organization that sells computer equipment and software packages to end users. Dealers may buy their products from distributors or directly from the producers.

Distributor

A distributor buys computer equipment and software directly from the producers and sells to dealers and systems houses. Distributors generally do not sell directly to end users.

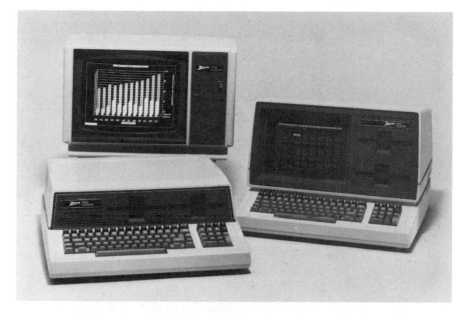

FIGURE 3–4 Electronic Spreadsheet with Graphics Application

OEM

*O*riginal *E*quipment *M*anufacturer. The term OEM is used differently in the computer industry compared to most other industries. In the computer industry most OEMs "manufacture" only plastic or metal labels and place these labels on computers and peripherals made by someone else. Many dealers who call themselves OEMs do not even bother with the labels. They assemble manufacturers' products (computers, peripherals, and software) to obtain a complete system.

Systems House, Systems Integrator

A dealer who sells a variety of computers, peripherals, and software. This dealer is able to package all the elements of a system to provide a wide variety of complete systems. Some of these vendors, correctly or incorrectly, call themselves OEMs.

FIGURE 3–5 Pie Chart Generated by Electronic Spreadsheet Package

Turnkey Vendor

A vendor who sells complete systems, including custom software and training. This vendor may be a systems integrator, represent a single brand, or provide complete systems from single sources.

Beta Site

An initial customer or customers for a new system. The system may be hardware, software, or both (turnkey). The beta site customers will usually receive special price, training, and support considerations.

4

SOFTWARE

Ninety percent of the problems in most business computer systems relate to the software, not the hardware.

A computer system is analogous to a home stereo system. The hardware is the equipment and blank tapes. The software is the music code, which you cannot see on the tapes—or in the case of radio, in the air. Since you cannot see this music code before the hardware processes it and turns it into music you can hear, you take it for granted. Without this "software," however, your "hardware" system is useless.

What if you bought a stereo "hardware" system and then found that the music you wanted was available only on a type of tape or record your machine could not play? A system, whether a stereo or a business computer, consists of all elements, both hardware and software, necessary to make the system perform.

Computer hardware is the "hard" or physical equipment that you can see and feel. It is the computer electronic devices and the box that houses these devices. It is also the TV screen, typewriter-like keyboard, printer, tape recorder/player and record (disk) player/recorder.

Hardware has received the notoriety and glamour because it can be seen. Tremendous hardware advances have been made in miniaturization, cost reductions, and increases in quality and capability. Hardware is also what is associated with brand names and large manufacturers and, consequently, the large advertising dollars.

Software is the part of a computer system that is "soft"— i.e., it cannot be seen or felt and can be easily altered or erased.

A software program is the final set of instructions between a computer and the user. The user enters data into the computer through the program, and the program instructs the computer how to process the data, make calculations, and then sort, summarize, and print the results.

The software tells the computer (hardware) how to process and file your information and give you the reports you need to manage your business. Good software can be easily changed, so that as a business grows and changes, the computer system can change and adjust.

A computer program (software) is a set of instructions. A computer will do exactly what it is told to do. It will interpret information precisely based on prior instructions. The computer becomes "programmed"—it cannot think.

OPERATING SYSTEM

The operating system consists of the initial software programs that enable the computer to understand and process instructions. This is the base dictionary of the system and includes communication, filing, and processing features. These features tell the various devices—printers, information TV screens, storage items, etc.—how to work together or how to simultaneously do independent jobs.

LANGUAGES

Languages are the next software step up from the operating system. The language is the dictionary or vocabulary that enables the computer to understand the programmers' instruction words.

Programs (sets of instructions) are written in a code or "language" that is understood by the computer. Assembly language is the program code that "talks" directly to the computer. This is the most difficult and detailed language. Higher level languages are translated into assembly code by a translator (called a compiler) built into the computer. Common high-level languages used in the 1970s were COBOL, FORTRAN, BASIC, and PASCAL. These languages, together with assembly language, are still used by skilled programmers.

Different operating systems and languages are best suited for different purposes. A business system may require large data input, filing and reporting volumes with simple calculations. An engineering or scientific computer may process little data but have lengthy and complex calculations.

Word processing and report generating systems (sometimes called data base management systems) are "languages" that enable the end users of a computer system to be programmers. These users, with relatively little training, can input data and instructions (programs) and create special files and reports.

Prior to the end of the 1970s, operating systems and languages were usually provided by the computer hardware manufacturers. Many manufacturers are now selling computers with operating systems and languages that have been developed by independent software companies to run on different hardware brands. New computers have been developed by many companies, including new ones, to operate on these common operating systems. Operating systems and languages, however, are not randomly interchangeable between hardware brands or even between models of a given brand.

Many new languages have been developed for special applications. In addition, many subroutines have been developed for common procedures using a given language. A programmer who is familiar with the library of subroutines and languages and who knows how to interrelate these tools can quickly build a finished program.

APPLICATION SOFTWARE

Application software is the last level of instructions preceding the user's information that are entered into and received from the computer system. The application software consists of the instructions (programs) that tell the computer how to receive and process application information.

Most business computer applications are of sufficient complexity to require a skilled and professional programmer to develop the software. An example would be processing product orders and sales. When order information is entered, the application software tells the computer how to find the related customer and product information, make calculations, print the order and invoice, and store the information for future cash receipts, statements, and sales analysis.

SOFTWARE PACKAGES

The previously mentioned languages, along with other techniques, have been used to develop what are called "software packages." Packages have many more constraints than the predecessor languages. The packages are useful, within their own constraints, for common situations or applications.

Every business, however, has unique requirements. Good packages can be modified. By using these packages or modules, a custom-appearing program can be quickly and efficiently created.

Numerous application software programs have been developed for resale. Good "package programs" are available at prices much lower than the cost for writing "custom" programs.

Packages for small computers typically sell for $100 to $1,000 and are available on tape cassettes or 3- to 8-inch floppy diskettes. The profit potential is obvious. Can you imagine making and selling stereo records for these prices? It appears that some people can, as there are now over 3,000 business entities (many are individuals utilizing only their homes) selling over 100,000 manufactured software packages.

Long development time, poor quality, low volume, weak user training, poor instruction documents, and/or high marketing costs have caused many of these businesses and products to fail. The successful products have been extremely profitable for their creators, and these products have had a dramatic impact on the small-computer industry.

Many computer industry analysts call these packages the tail that waves the dog. Many people buy the computer for the package rather than vice versa. This is the recommended approach, as we have strongly emphasized—*buy the software first!*

The software packages that have had the greatest impact for small-computer users are the electronic spreadsheet, graphics, word processing, and data base management systems (DBMS), and the accounting function packages. These packages are actually very high-level languages. They enable the user to write a custom program for a specific application with *relative* ease. (We stress the relative, because writing such programs is usually not as easy as the sellers make it out to be, and it takes learning, skill, and understanding to utilize these powerful tools.) It takes skill and knowledge to know what package to use and how to use that package for a given application. When the right package is selected, some applications can be programmed with less than one-tenth the time and cost it would have taken three years ago.

ELECTRONIC SPREADSHEETS

The electronic spreadsheet packages enable the user to create and update tables. This is especially useful in financial, sales, personnel or production forecasting, planning, and budgeting. Relations between rows or columns can be easily programmed. Simple programming codes and their interpretation are displayed on the screen or are in a brief manual. Growth rates can be used to automatically calculate items. Changes (what-ifs) can be easily compared. A few of the popular spreadsheet packages are VisiCalc, SuperCalc, MicroPlan, MagiCalc, and CalcStar.

Many experts call VisiCalc the tool that made the personal computer market what it is today. VisiCalc is the largest selling package program in history. The package was introduced in 1979, and more than 200,000 copies were sold the first two years. The personal professional computer hardware phenomenon started in 1976 and 1977 and was led by Apple and Radio Shack. Radio Shack entered the computer business in 1977 with an existing distribution and a large potential personal computer customer base. Apple started from nothing in 1975. Both companies' products were initially well accepted because they offered a low-cost product that a technical specialist could program using a version of BASIC or another standard programming language.

The initial customers for these personal computers were primarily engineering and math-oriented people who wrote their own programs in traditional languages. VisiCalc was introduced in 1979 for the Apple computer. A Radio Shack version was introduced shortly thereafter. After VisiCalc was introduced, the sales of personal computers exploded.

Apple and Radio Shack computer sales for the last four years were as follows:

	APPLE	RADIO SHACK
1979	$ 75,000,000	$150,000,000
1980	165,000,000	220,000,000
1981	401,000,000	460,000,000
1982	710,000,000	600,000,000

A version of VisiCalc is now available on most general-purpose, single-user computers. There are now approximately one hundred low-cost electronic spreadsheet packages (sometimes called "visiclones" and "calcalikes") available. Many of these newer packages contain improvements that give the package more power or make it easier to use for certain specialized types of applications. VisiCalc continues to be the leading seller, and many VisiCalc users meet to exchange application ideas and help each other solve problems using VisiCalc.

A person shopping for an electronic spreadsheet package and computer system should carefully evaluate the available products in relation to the application needs. The ongoing vendor and/or user group support can have a significant effect on the success and usefulness of the system.

VisiCalc and other electronic spreadsheet packages have enabled many users to become "programmers," putting their own personal computer to immediate and productive use. These packages are actually very high-level languages that are more structured (limited) and have fewer commands than traditional, more general-purpose, languages such as BASIC, COBOL, FORTRAN, and PASCAL. Such languages include many structured common commands (program instruction codes) within the package, each in turn including a chain of preprogrammed commands or many subcommands. Therefore, each step or command in an electronic spreadsheet application program requires only a fraction of the number of commands that would be required with a traditional language.

Word processing and electronic spreadsheets are the most popular uses for single-user (personal) computers. Dedicated word processing computers started to become popular in the mid 1970s and provided the first improved productivity justification for the single-user computer. The early personal word processing computers cost $15,000 to $20,000, but could generate a 50 to 100 percent increase in productivity. This "modest" productivity increase required nearly full computer utilization in order to justify the cost of the computer.

In many applications an electronic spreadsheet computer that costs less than $5,000 for hardware and software can generate a ten- to fifty-fold increase in productivity. The computer, therefore, can pay for itself in one year if it is effectively used only fifteen minutes a day to save two hours of a $25,000-per-year professional's time.

Word processing packages are for standard paragraphs of text. Both word processing and spreadsheet packages provide for easy editing and rearranging of information and reprinting of corrected, perfect copies of the information stored in the computer. The electronic spreadsheet packages have the same benefits as word processing systems, except that the spreadsheet packages are for standard matrices (columns and rows) of information.

The tremendous increase in productivity that an electronic spreadsheet computer can generate comes from rapid speeds of calculation. Increased productivity power comes from recalculating complex relationships after base information has been changed. Calculating, even using sophisticated electronic calculators, is one of the things humans do slowest. Electronic computers calculate extremely fast. In addition, humans tend to forget all the relationships in a complex table, or they neglect to follow the previously established procedures. Manually prepared tables may require extensive checking to assure accuracy.

Additional benefits of a spreadsheet package can be achieved by using common formats for multiple units of an organization. Many systems can automatically perform tedious consolidations.

The most common application for electronic spreadsheets is financial budgeting and forecasting. An example of this type of table or model, "Pro Forma Financial Statements," is shown in Fig. 4–1. Anyone involved with forecasting knows that it is a very dynamic activity. Forecasts are based on varying assumptions and probabilities. Many times, the users of forecasts will want to see the forecast model tested with various probabilities and "what if" assumptions. Before the existence of electronic spreadsheets, managers would frustrate financial analysts with apparently simple changes in assumptions that would result in tedious hours of recalculation.

Any activity requiring a standard form or format and involving arithmetic relationships of numbers within the form can be programmed using an electronic spreadsheet package. A list of some of the popular applications in addition to financial forecasting and budgeting follows. The information in the rows and columns is described.

1. Investment portfolio
   Rows: List of investments.
   Columns: Date of purchase, purchase price, current value, percentage increase, annualized percentage increase.
   Totals: All items plus a weighted average performance index.
2. Product cost and price lists
   Rows: List of products.
   Columns: Cost parameters, product components, calculated cost, price list at given margins or margins at given prices.
3. Expense accounts
   Rows: Expense items, subtotals, advances, net due.
   Columns: Dates with amounts.
4. Sales calls analysis
   Rows: Customers.
   Columns: Last ten calls, average frequency, days since last call, date next call due in relation to average frequency.
5. Production schedule
   Rows: Jobs and units.
   Columns: Workstations with dates completed or scheduled.
   Summary: Volume by workstation, date.

Additional applications without row and column descriptions are:

1. Analysis of golf, bowling, or other sports scores with moving averages or handicap ratings.

	1982 QTR AVG	1983 1ST QTR	1983 2ND QTR	1983 3RD QTR	1983 4TH QTR	1983 TOTAL	1984 TOTAL	1985 TOTAL
PRO FORMA FINANCIAL STATEMENTS 1983–1985 ($ Totals in Thousands)								Page 1
SALES:								
Units	90.0	150.0	250.0	350.0	500.0	1,250.0	2,500.0	6,000.0
Avg. Price	$1,100.0	$1,200.0	$1,200.0	$1,200.0	$1,200.0	$1,200.0	$1,200.0	$1,200.0
Sales ($ 000)	$99.0	$180.0	$300.0	$420.0	$600.0	$1,500.0	$3,000.0	$7,200.0
DIRECT COSTS:								
MATERIAL:								
Per Unit	560.0	560.0	550.0	540.0	530.0	540.4	510.0	500.0
Total ($ 000)	50.4	84.0	137.5	189.0	265.0	675.5	1,275.0	3,000.0
% Sales	50.9%	46.7%	45.8%	45.0%	44.2%	45.0%	42.5%	41.7%
LABOR:								
# Directly Employed	10.0	10.0	10.0	11.0	16.0	11.8	20.0	50.0
Avg. Monthly Wages	1,200.0	1,200.0	1,200.0	1,200.0	1,200.0	1,200.0	1,200.0	1,200.0
Total ($ 000)	36.0	36.0	36.0	39.6	57.6	169.2	288.0	720.0
TOTAL	86.4	120.0	173.5	228.6	322.6	844.7	1,563.0	3,720.0
Percent Sales	87.3%	66.7%	57.8%	54.4%	53.8%	56.3%	52.1%	51.7%
GROSS MARGIN	12.6	60.0	126.5	191.4	277.4	655.3	1,437.0	3,480.0
Percent Sales	12.7%	33.3%	42.2%	45.6%	46.2%	43.7%	47.9%	48.3%
FACTORY OVERHEAD:								
Supplies	2.1	2.1	2.1	2.1	2.1	8.4	7.0	13.0
Insurance	4.5	4.5	4.5	4.5	4.5	18.0	15.0	25.0
Rent	4.7	4.7	4.7	4.7	4.7	18.8	19.0	25.0
Utilities	1.1	1.1	1.1	1.1	1.1	4.4	6.0	10.0
License	3.0	3.0	7.5	7.5	7.5	25.5	2.5	
Other & Misc.	1.5	3.0	3.0	3.0	3.0	12.0	15.0	20.0
Total	16.9	18.4	22.9	22.9	22.9	87.1	64.5	93.0
GROSS PROFIT	−4.3	41.6	103.6	168.5	254.5	568.2	1,372.5	3,387.0
Percent Sales	−4.3%	23.1%	34.5%	40.1%	42.4%	37.9%	45.8%	47.0%

FIGURE 4–1 Electronic Spreadsheet Table

PRO FORMA FINANCIAL STATEMENTS   Page 2
1983-1985 ($ Totals in Thousands)

	1982 QTR AVG	1983 1ST QTR	1983 2ND QTR	1983 3RD QTR	1983 4TH QTR	1983 TOTAL	1984 TOTAL	1985 TOTAL
SALES	$99.0	$180.0	$300.0	$420.0	$600.0	$1,500.0	$3,000.0	$7,200.0
COST OF SALES	103.3	138.4	196.4	251.5	345.5	931.8	1,627.5	3,813.0
GROSS PROFIT	−4.3	41.6	103.6	168.5	254.5	568.2	1,372.5	3,387.0
SELLING & MARKETING:								
Commissions	9.9	18.0	30.0	42.0	60.0	150.0	300.0	720.0
Advertising	5.0	9.0	15.0	21.0	30.0	75.0	150.0	360.0
Other & Misc.	5.0	9.0	15.0	21.0	30.0	75.0	150.0	360.0
Total	19.8	36.0	60.0	84.0	120.0	300.0	600.0	1,440.0
Percent Sales	20.0%	20.0%	20.0%	20.0%	20.0%	20.0%	20.0%	20.0%
GENERAL & ADMINISTRATIVE:								
Production Manager	6.0	6.0	6.0	6.0	6.0	24.0	36.0	45.0
Engineer		8.0	8.0	8.0	8.0	32.0	45.0	60.0
Office Salaries	6.0	8.0	8.0	8.0	8.0	32.0	48.0	72.0
Supplies	1.5	1.5	1.5	1.5	1.5	6.0	8.0	14.0
Legal & Accounting	1.5	10.0	3.0	3.0	3.0	19.0	15.0	20.0
Telephone	1.2	1.5	1.5	1.5	1.5	6.0	8.0	12.0
Interest		4.9	9.5	12.4	15.2	42.0	31.8	−22.7
Other & Misc.	1.5	2.0	2.0	2.0	2.0	8.0	10.0	15.0
Total	17.7	41.9	39.5	42.4	45.2	169.0	201.6	215.2
Percent Sales	17.9%	23.3%	13.2%	10.1%	7.5%	11.3%	6.7%	3.0%
PROFIT BEFORE TAXES	−41.8	−36.3	4.1	42.1	89.3	99.2	570.9	1,731.8
Provision For Taxes		−18.1	2.0	21.1	44.7	49.6	′285.5	865.9
NET PROFIT	$−41.8	$−18.1	$2.0	$21.1	$44.7	$49.6	$285.5	$865.9
Percent Sales	−73.4%	−10.1%	0.7%	5.0%	7.4%	3.3%	9.5%	12.0%

FIGURE 4–1 (continued) Electronic Spreadsheet Table

	1982 QTR AVG	1983 1ST QTR	1983 2ND QTR	1983 3RD QTR	1983 4TH QTR	1983 TOTAL	1984 TOTAL	1985 TOTAL
			PRO FORMA FINANCIAL STATEMENTS	1983–1985 ($ Totals in Thousands)				Page 3
BALANCE SHEET:								
ASSETS:								
Accounts Receivable	70.0	120.6	201.0	281.4	402.0	402.0	500.0	1,200.0
Inventory	150.0	84.0	137.5	189.0	265.0	265.0	318.8	750.0
Property & Equipment	20.0	20.0	20.0	20.0	20.0	20.0	50.0	100.0
Total	$240.0	$224.6	$358.5	$490.4	$687.0	$687.0	$868.8	$2,050.0
LIABILITIES & EQUITY:								
Accounts Payable	$45.0	$72.1	$98.6	$126.0	$170.2	$170.2	$202.4	$455.7
Taxes Payable		−18.1	−16.1	5.0	49.6	49.6	235.8	580.5
Credit Line		108.8	212.1	274.5	337.6	337.6	15.6	−266.9
Invested Equity		80.0	80.0	80.0	80.0	80.0	80.0	80.0
Retained Earnings		−18.1	−16.1	5.0	49.6	49.6	335.0	1,200.8
Total	$45.0	$224.6	$358.5	$490.4	$687.0	$687.0	$868.8	$2,050.0

FIGURE 4–1 (continued) Electronic Spreadsheet Table

2. Product part lists.
3. Real estate buyer/seller closing statements.
4. Attendance and grade analysis by student.
5. Physical inventory list and extension.
6. Financial statement analysis, including profit center allocations and various ratios.
7. Engineering tables.
8. Fixed asset and depreciation tables.
9. Loan amortization tables.
10. Staffing patterns or schedules.
11. Insurance payments and cash value for alternative payment plans and types of payments.
12. Projected retirement budget and cash flow.
13. Tax planning.

The uses of electronic spreadsheets seem to be limited only by the imagination of the users.

In a spreadsheet table, model, or form, each element of information within the format is called a cell. With VisiCalc, SuperCalc, and most other packages, each cell is defined by the row number (1 to 254) and the column letter(s) (A to Z plus AA to AZ plus BA to BK) for 63 columns. In the example of Fig. 4–1, "Page 1" and the title are in rows 1 through 4, with "Page 1" in column I and the title in columns B through F. The row titles are all in column A. A table is established by entering the appropriate titles in the appropriate cells by moving the cursor on the screen to the appropriate cell and typing the appropriate information or calculation command. The user can see the model being created on the screen.

The best procedure for computer modeling or planning is to first draw a rough skeleton with a pencil. The key to success in developing easy-to-program, -revise, -read, and -use electronic spreadsheet models is proper advance planning. The creator of the model should write the formulas for column and row or cell relations and then type the information and commands into the computer. This would be similar to giving step-by-step instructions to a clerk. When these instructions are completed, the model will have been created, and the computer will not forget the relational instructions.

In the table of Fig. 4–1, the user would first create the "skeleton" by typing in all the report, row, and column titles along with lines and symbols for subtotals and totals. Base data are then entered in the appropriate cells, and commands are entered for calculations. A sample of some of the commands for the "Pro Forma Financial Statements" example is shown in Table 4–1. (The actual symbols and the format of the commands will differ with the package used.)

In the model, the required financing (credit line) is calculated, and interest is automatically revised, which in turn revises the profit and credit line requirements. Several pushes of a button requesting recalculation may be required to complete the looping process so that all items are properly computed.

After the table is completed, the user may revise some of the base data, e.g., sales units, and request recalculation. After the user is satisfied with the model as seen on the computer screen, the model may be printed. The model can be further revised, or tried with different assumptions. Any model may be saved on the disk for future use or consolidation.

The "Pro Forma Financial Statements" model was actually created using the spreadsheet package MicroPlan. The MicroPlan

Table 4-1
VisiCalc®-Type Commands

CELL DESCRIPTION (CURSOR)

ROW	COLUMN	COMMAND
(11) Units	(G) 1983 Total	=SUM (C11 . . . F11)
(14) Sales ($000)	(B-I) All Data	=(B-I) 11 × 12/1000
(14) Sales ($000)	(G) 1983 Total	= SUM (C14 . . . F14)
(12) Avg. Price	(G) 1983 Total	=G14/G11
(20) Total ($000)	(B-I) All Data	=(B-I)11 × (B-I) 18/1000
(20) Total ($000)	(G) 1983 Total	=SUM (C20 . . . F20)
(18) Per Unit	(G) 1983 Total	=G20/G11
(22) % Sales	(B-I) All Data	=(B-I)20/(B-I)14 × 100
(25) # Direct Employees	(G) 1983 Total	=SUM (C25 . . . F25)/4
.	.	.
.	.	.
.	.	.
(60) SALES	(B-I) All Data	=(B-I)14
.	.	.
.	.	.
.	.	.
(109) Accounts Receivable (C-F)	1983 Qtrs	=(C-F)14 × .67
.	.	.
.	.	.
.	.	.

package was developed (by Chang Laboratories, Inc.) specifically for financial planning. The package lacks some of the versatility of VisiCalc and other packages, but for this type of financial planning model, it can develop tables and programs much faster.

In the "Pro Forma Financial Statements" model, the titles, pages, and column and row headings are entered along with formatting ($ signs, underlining, spacing, etc.) commands. Base data, exluding totals and items such as percents and commissions that are a function of base data, are entered next. A program is then written to perform all calculations. In the MicroPlan programming language, all commands are entered with two- or three-digit reference numbers and numerical parameters. This makes the programming very fast for most financial analysts, since they can work using the ten-key numerical portion of the keyboard primarily. The system will print the program, with the computer providing table location, command, and parameter descriptions. This printout provides excellent documentation. The program printout for the "Pro Forma Financial Statements" model is shown in Fig. 4–2.

In this example it took approximately one hour for a financial analyst to set up the table (three pages) and another hour to write the 67-step program. The analyst can now change any base data items, rerun the program and print a new three-page table all in a few minutes.

GRAPHICS

Graphics packages provide for the plotting of data and the production of bar charts or pie charts. These packages are often interfaced with an electronic spreadsheet package. Color graphics are also available.

Black and white graphs can be printed using a standard dot-matrix printer. Color graphics require a special, expensive printer-plotter. Many of these devices are computerized drafting/drawing machines.

Good graphics software packages, prior to 1982, were usually expensive (over $10,000) and required special equipment. Graphics packages for small computers are achieving rapid improvements in quality and decreases in prices.

WORD PROCESSING

Word processing started to become popular in the mid 1970s. The early word processing computer systems were specially designed only for this application. A word processing system in the mid 1970s usually cost $15,000 to $20,000. The system included a CRT screen, keyboard, letter-quality printer, word processing software, manuals, and training. Data were stored on small floppy disks or tape cassettes. Most systems were single-user systems.

The main advantage of a dedicated word processing computer is that all features of the system are designed for one purpose. The companies who make and sell these systems usually

STEP	DATA POINTER	COMMAND	PARAMETERS
1	ROW 4(Sales ($ 000)) ←	COL RANGE	COLS 1 TO 8
2	ROW 4(Sales ($ 000)) ←	L2*L3/1000	
3	ROW 8(Total ($ 000)) ←	L2*L7/1000	
4	ROW 11(# Directly Employed) ←	COL RANGE	COLS 2 TO 5
5	ROW 13(Total ($ 000)) ←	L11*L12*3/1000	
6	ROW 13(Total ($ 000)) ←	COL RANGE	COLS 7 TO 8
7	ROW 13(Total ($ 000)) ←	L11*L12*12/1000	
8	COL 6(1983 TOTAL) ←	SUM	COLS 2 TO 5
9	COL 7(1984 TOTAL) ←	COL RANGE	COLS 1 TO 8
10	ROW 3(Avg. Price) ←	L4/L2*1000	
11	ROW 7(Per Unit) ←	L8/L2*1000	
12	ROW 9(% Sales) ←	L8/L4*100	
13	ROW 14(TOTAL) ←	ADD	ROW=8 ROW=13
14	ROW 15(Percent Sales) ←	L14/L4*100	
15	ROW 16(GROSS MARGIN) ←	SUBTRACT	ROW=4 ROW=14
16	ROW 17(Percent Sales) ←	L16/L4*100	
17	ROW 25(Total) ←	SUM	ROWS 19 TO 24
18	ROW 26(GROSS PROFIT) ←	SUBTRACT	ROW=16 ROW=25
19	ROW 27(Percent Sales) ←	L26/L4*100	
20	ROW 28(SALES) ←	GET	ROW=4
21	ROW 30(GROSS PROFIT) ←	GET	ROW=26
22	ROW 29(COST OF SALES) ←	SUBTRACT	ROW=28 ROW=30
23	ROW 32(Commissions) ←	MULT K	K=0.1 ROW=4
24	ROW 33(Advertising) ←	MULT K	K=0.05 ROW=4
25	ROW 34(Other & Misc.) ←	MULT K	K=0.05 ROW=4
26	ROW 35(Total) ←	SUM	ROWS 32 TO 34
27	ROW 36(Percent Sales) ←	L35/L4*100	
28	ROW 46(Total) ←	SUM	ROWS 38 TO 45
29	ROW 47(Percent Sales) ←	L46/L4*100	
30	ROW 48(PROFIT BEFORE TAXES) ←	L30-L35-L46	
31	ROW 49(Provision For Taxes) ←	COL RANGE	COLS 2 TO 8
32	ROW 49(Provision For Taxes) ←	K PCT	50% ROW=48
33	ROW 50(NET PROFIT) ←	SUBTRACT	ROW=48 ROW=49
34	ROW 51(Percent Sales) ←	L50/L4*100	
35	ROW 52(BALANCE SHEET:) ←	COL RANGE	COLS 2 TO 5

FIGURE 4–2 MicroPlan Program for Pro Forma Financial Statements

STEP	DATA POINTER		COMMAND	PARAMETERS
36	ROW 54(	Accounts Receivable ←	K PCT	67% ROW=4
37	ROW 55(	Inventory) ←	GET	ROW=8
38	ROW 56(	Property & Equipment) ←	20	
39	ROW 57(	Total) ←	SUM	ROWS 54 TO 56
40	ROW 59(	Accounts Payable) ←	(L4-L48)/3	
41	ROW 60(	Taxes Payable) ←	CUMULATE	K=0 ROW=49
42	ROW 63(	Retained Earnings) ←	CUMULATE	K=0 ROW=50
43	ROW 61(	Credit Line) ←	L57-L59-L60-L62-L63	
44	ROW 64(	Total) ←	SUM	ROWS 59 TO 63
45	ROW 44(	Interest) ←	K PCT	4.5% ROW=61
46	ROW 45(	Other & Misc.) ←	ROW RANGE	ROWS 38 TO 65
47	ROW 1(SALES:) ←		ROW RANGE	ROWS 54 TO 64
48	COL 6(1983 TOTAL) ←		GET	COL=5
49	COL 7(1984 TOTAL) ←		COL RANGE	COLS 7 TO 8
50	ROW 54(	Accounts Receivable) ←	DIV K	K=6 ROW=4
51	ROW 55(	Inventory) ←	DIV K	K=4 ROW=8
52	ROW 57(	Total) ←	SUM	ROWS 54 TO 56
53	ROW 59(	Accounts Payable) ←	(L4-L48)/12	
54			60,7 ← V49,7-V49,6	
55			60,8 ← V49,8-V49,7	
56	ROW 65 ←		COL RANGE	COLS 6 TO 8
57	ROW 65 ←		GET	ROW=49
58	ROW 65 ←		COL RANGE	COLS 7 TO 8
59	ROW 63(	Retained Earnings) ←	CUMULATE	K=0 ROW=65
60	ROW 61(	Credit Line) ←	L57-L59-L60-L62-L63	
61	ROW 64(	Total) ←	SUM	ROWS 59 TO 63
62			44,7 ← (V61,6+V61,7)*.18/2	
63			44,8 ← (V61,7+V61,8)*.18/2	
64			11,6 ← (V11,2+V11,3+V11,4+V11,5)/4	
65			12,6 ← V13,6*1000/V11,6/12	
66	ROW 47(	Percent Sales) ←	ROW RANGE	ROWS 1 TO 64
67	ROW 47(	Percent Sales) ←	COL RANGE	COLS 1 TO 8

FIGURE 4-2 (continued) MicroPlan Program for Pro Forma Financial Statements

provide good specialized training and support. Some of the more prominent word processing specialty companies are CPT Corporation, Lanier Business Products, Lexitron (subsidiary of Raytheon), Micom (subsidiary of Philips Information Systems), and MDS Systems (subsidiary of Mohawk Data Systems).

The specialty word processors can be single-user systems (like personal computers) or "shared logic systems." A shared logic system has a central computer, with different word processing operators being able to access a central file of documents and other information.

We have defined a personal computer as a computer that can do only one thing at one time for one person. Most dedicated word processing computers fit this definition.

A word processor is electronically and physically no different from any other business or personal computer. A computer becomes a word processor with a software package. Word processors were formerly separate hardware because of the complexity of the software and special features of the hardware required to utilize the software.

Word processing software packages are now available for most small computers. These packages enable the user to insert items, rearrange text, and make corrections. The system will automatically center, left and right justify, space proportionally, number pages, and perform many other features. "Boilerplate" documents, such as wills or proposals, are easily customized. More sophisticated packages will beep when a word is entered that is not in the spelling dictionary. Some packages enable automatic numeric calculations in columns embedded in the text.

Most systems have a supplemental mailing list package that can integrate with the word processing package. The computer can sort and pick out individuals or groups from the list. Labels can be printed. The selected sublist can be merged with a boilerplate letter to create personalized letters.

The word processing operator becomes a programmer creating a program for a special document. A few of the popular word processing packages include Apple-Writer, EasyWriter, WordStar, Magic Wand and WordPro.

Features and quality vary considerably among various word processing packages and equipment. Most word processing is now performed on computers that can be used for other purposes, either personal computers or multiuser general business computers. Most suppliers of personal computers and small-business computers now provide word processing capabilities with their systems.

The word processing capability for personal computers is usually provided on diskettes. The computer operator inserts a word processing diskette, and the computer becomes a word processor. If the operator wishes to do something else, such as accounting, the job must be stopped and diskettes switched.

Small-business computers, which are larger than personal computers and provide for simultaneous multiuser operation, usually have larger capacity hard disks rather than the small diskettes. These hard disks may contain the programs or code for all applications. In such a case, one operator may be doing word processing while another operator is doing accounting. In addition, the word processing operator may use data from the accounting system to create special reports. Systems with these features may be slower than a dedicated computer for a specific function. Again, quality and features vary considerably among suppliers.

Definitions of the different types of computers are beginning to lose their distinctions. The features that formerly defined one type have expanded and blended into the features that define other types. This is also true of word processors. A single-user word processing computer is a personal computer. A multiuser or shared logic word processor is a small-business microcomputer or minicomputer. Some general-purpose personal computers now have multiuser capabilities, so these computers are becoming small-business computers at personal computer prices. The specialty word processing companies previously mentioned are adding general business features, including arithmetic and numerical column functions, to their word processing systems. Electronic spreadsheets and data base management and accounting packages integrated with their standard word processing are now being offered.

The best way to evaluate the various word processing packages or dedicated systems is to try them. Prior to making comparative tests of various word processing systems, you should prepare a sample problem. This will be the type of document you normally prepare, and the test problems should be problems often incurred. When you test each system, you will process your document and rearrange text, insert items, and perform other functions. You will get a feel for each system and its features.

The advantages and disadvantages of each major type of word processor are given in the following list.

1. General-purpose personal computer
   Advantage: Low cost, flexibility.
   Disadvantage: Many have fewer specialty features and less vendor word processing expertise and support.
2. Dedicated word processor
   Advantage: Usually more features and vendor expertise and support.
   Disadvantage: Lack of flexibility.
3. General-purpose multiuser business computer
   Advantage: Flexibility, integrated information files.
   Disadvantage: May have fewer specialty features and less vendor word processing expertise and support and may be slower than more specialized computers.

DATA BASE MANAGEMENT SYSTEMS (DBMSs)

A DBMS system differs from an electronic spreadsheet system in that it provides for unstructured formats. Selected reports can be obtained from a large file of information or transactions. Data bases (files) can be cross-referenced so that master information for an item can be printed with sorted and/or summarized activity (transactions).

A sample of a DBMS instruction (program) is:

```
LIST SALESINV WHERE SALESINV
GR 100 BY CUST DESC SALES,
INVNO DATE SALES COST
GP% = SALES/(SALES-COST)*100,
TOTAL SALES COST GP% CUST,
AVG SALES CUST
```

This program would list sales invoices that are over $100 by customer in descending-sales-amount order and show the invoice number, date, sales, cost, and gross-profit-percent for each invoice and calculate the total sales, cost, and gross-profit-percent and average sales per customer for these invoices. An example report for this program is shown as Fig. 4–3.

The DBMS packages often are named with the computer manufacturer's name followed by a hyphen and the term "DBMS," e.g., DEC-DBMS. There are many interestingly named DBMS packages, such as dBASE II, FMS-80, MDBS III, SUP-R-FILER, IMAGE, ENGLISH, IDOL, CONTROL, REQUEST, INFO-80, PRISM, and many more.

ACCOUNTING PACKAGES

Accounting packages process accounting transactions and print checks, invoices, purchase orders, and other documents and reports. These packages include general ledger and financial statements, sales and accounts receivable, checks and accounts payable, purchasing, order entry and backlog, inventory, professional time and billing, and payroll.

Accounting packages have a tremendous range in price and

CUSTOMER		INVOICE NUMBER	INVOICE DATE	SALES AMOUNT	COST	GROSS PROFIT PERCENT
Adams Company		1721	5/01/83	$563.72	$321.11	43.0%
		2626	5/16/83	471.88	283.77	39.9
		1908	5/11/83	273.21	181.62	33.5
		3121	5/28/83	101.01	56.28	44.3
	Total			1,409.82	842.78	40.2
	Average			352.46		
Baker Tool		1816	5/09/83	223.21	143.66	35.6
Martin Electric		1211	4/11/83	321.18	191.89	40.3
		2622	5/16/83	182.16	113.56	37.7
	Total			503.34	305.45	39.3
	Average			251.67		
Zeda Supply		2333	5/14/83	132.72	68.99	48.0
GRAND TOTAL				$2,269.09	$1,360.88	40.0%
AVERAGE, 8 INVOICES				$ 283.64		

FIGURE 4–3 Data Base Management System Report

features. Some of the packages do not work in most businesses. What one salesperson calls an accounts payable system may not be what another person expects of an accounts payable system. The business accounting packages should provide management with information like easy-to-read summary reports, including key ratios. Many of the packages are merely bookkeeping systems that make the computer an electronic posting and bookkeeping machine and do not utilize all the electronic power and programming tools and techniques that are currently available.

The better systems will be "parameter driven." With these systems, the user can input parameters (again, write a "program") to create special reports, custom formats, and special features. A user should have the assistance of a professional accountant, experienced in computer systems, to help set up the system. A poorly designed structure (coding system) will abuse the features of the system and can cause numerous problems in future use and corrections.

Some computer salespeople will say that with their computer and accounting packages, a business user can eliminate its outside professional accountant. That is not true. A good system will, however, substantially reduce the outside accounting costs. A good accounting firm will welcome this reduction, as the firm can do more professional work instead of the tedious, low-profit posting and sorting activities that are very efficiently performed by the computer.

PURCHASING SOFTWARE

The vast majority of software packages are sold by dealers who do not know how to use the packages they are selling. Many packages are sold in a cellophane bag in a retail store. The buyer does not know what is inside until after he has paid for the package. Do not buy a package this way if you have problems following toy manufacturers' assembly instructions.

We cannot stress enough the wide variations in package features and quality. Do not buy a package just because of the name and function. Know what you want the package to do and what features are important to you. Shop around and see the package in operation in a real environment. Talk to other users. The business and people from whom you buy a package are very important.

Package software offers very powerful, inexpensive tools. There are thousands of packages, and the numbers are increasing every day. There are probably some packages which you can use very effectively, but there are thousands that will give you many headaches.

Purchasing software is usually cheaper than hiring a programmer to develop the software. Good business systems software vendors sell package software, modify package software, and develop custom-appearing software using the previously mentioned methods.

If you do not own a business computer system and are contemplating the purchase of one—BUY THE SOFTWARE FIRST!

If you already own a computer you will have fewer options for software, and the software will be more expensive than if purchased in conjunction with the hardware.

In any case, the key to success in application software and programmer productivity is management. If your business does not possess the proper skills, or the managers who do possess these skills do not have enough time, then the best investment you can make is in quality contract management.

SOFTWARE COSTS

There has been a great deal written about the price of hardware going down while the price of software is going up. This is because many businesses are spending ten or more times the amount they need to be spending for software.

Most large businesses are reluctant to disclose the cost of their failures. Many times, the budget for software costs is more than for hardware costs and thus indicative of the problems.

The U.S. government has disclosed some of its problems. There was a comma missing in a program for the Apollo rocket. It crashed. It cost $15 million.

A recent report to Congress by the Comptroller, General Accounting Office (GAO), report FGMSD-80-4, November 9, 1979, cited: Of nine software contracts examined, totaling $6.8 million software never used cost $5.2 million (76.5%), software extensively reworked before use cost $1.3 million (19.1%), and software actually used cost $300,000 (4.4%).

The government has utilized some of the so-called most sophisticated management and project control techniques used by larger businesses and advocated by large consulting firms and university faculties. Many of the management techniques used in larger organizations involve committees, often called "steering committees." We do not recommend these committees. They result in unnecessary expenses (including consulting), cause delays and inefficiencies, and are usually an excuse for weak management.

With the recent increases in technology and tools available, a business' computer software and hardware annual expenses should be declining, unless the business is growing extremely rapidly. The computer system department manager should be getting projects done on time and within budget. When this is happening, there is no need or demand for a committee. In fact, a manager who is achieving these results is not usually working for a committee.

We have developed a checkpoint management procedure that is in tune with the current state-of-the-art, low-cost, quality software. The steps in this method relate to the same common sense management principles necessary for any successful technical and capital expenditure business project.

STEPS FOR SUCCESS—
OVERALL MANAGEMENT

The steps for implementing a successful computer system application software project are to:

1. Know what you want the project to accomplish, and define this in writing.
2. Know how this project will affect and interrelate with all other application software systems that currently are, or will be in the future, in the total computer system.
3. Have one manager, who is not the programmer, in charge of the project.
4. Contract with a programmer who is a specialist in this type of project, to complete the project.

5. Pay for services on a milestone basis.
6. Make sure that all work is thoroughly documented so that another programmer can later modify this application or interrelate it with other applications.

A skilled programmer will utilize the best tools available in the large and growing software library. If you have a programmer or programmers on your staff, your choices will be more limited. You need to manage your programmers very carefully and make sure that they are following proper procedure as closely as possible.

STEPS FOR SUCCESS— PROGRAMMER

A skilled programmer creating application software will pick the best packages, subroutines, languages, and operating system. This professional skill requires specialization. A professional programmer is a specialist and works best with certain applications, languages, and operating systems.

Success in a business computer application, therefore, requires management attention in initially picking the right programmer. If the business management is not familiar with assessing the skills of programmers, the management should first pick a skilled independent advisor or consultant.

From a programmer's point of view, the steps for developing a successful program are the same as before, plus:

1. Define the project and all current and potential future software systems interrelations.
2. Select the best packages and application subroutine packages.
3. Select the best language for the previous items.
4. Select the best operating system for the previous items.
5. Select the best hardware for the previous items.

5

TYPES
OF COMPUTERS

One of the most common questions from computer users and potential purchasers relates to personal or desk-top computers versus microcomputers versus minicomputers versus mainframe computers. Basically, they are all the same, and there is no clear distinction or break. There are wide variations in features and prices between brands. Generally, however, more expensive computers can handle more information and will have more features important to a business environment. In general terms, personal computers are priced from $500 to $15,000, microcomputer systems are priced from $10,000 to $50,000, minicomputer systems are priced from $20,000 to $1 million, and mainframes are priced from $500,000 to more than $10 million.

Larger, more expensive computers are able to perform more complex activities and simultaneously access more information for more users at a faster speed. Some of the generally accepted criteria for the different classifications of computers are shown in Table 5–1.

MAINFRAMES

Mainframes have been the mainstay of the data processing industry. Most large organizations of more than 5,000 employees

Table 5–1
TYPE OF COMPUTER
(Classification Criteria)

	PERSONAL	MICRO-COMPUTER	MINI-COMPUTER	MAINFRAME
Size	Thin board in CRT	Desk-top Box	Refrigerator	Multiple Cabinets
Price:				
Minimum $	500	10,000	20,000	500,000
Maximum $	15,000	50,000	1,000,000	10,000,000 +
Memory:				
Minimum K	16	64	64	256
Maximum K	128	512	2,000	16,000
On-line Disk:				
Minimum MB	.1	.5	10	400
Maximum MB	5	70	2,000	50,000 +
Maximum Number of Simultaneous Users	1	16	100	Unlimited
Speed	Very Fast	Faster	Still Faster	Incredible
Word Size:				
Minimum bits	8	8	16	32
Maximum bits	16	16	32	64

have one or more mainframe computers. A mainframe consists of complex and multiple central processing units within the computer configuration. The CPU word size is usually 32 bits. Mainframes have large memory storage and program space and have the ability to add numerous printers, data readers, terminals, disk drives, tape drives, and communication ports. They can process very large volumes of data for many users at many locations. Mainframe prices may range from $500,000 to many millions of dollars. Mainframes are an expensive investment and may have to operate 24 hours a day to justify their existence.

MINICOMPUTERS

Minicomputers are the next level of computers and are smaller than the giant mainframes. Some minicomputers are more powerful than the smaller mainframes. Some that are on the market have a 32-bit word size and 4 megabytes of memory. Most of today's minicomputers are more powerful than the mainframes of ten years ago.

Minicomputers generally range in price from $20,000 to $1 million. The minicomputer is generally smaller than a mainframe, has more than one CPU chip, and has a CPU word size of 16 or 32 bits. Older model minicomputers have 8-bit words. When minicomputers first appeared in the late 1960s and early 1970s, they were extremely popular with businesses that had mainframes but had applications requiring a dedicated computer. Minicomputers were placed in manufacturing environments for numerical machine and process control. They were also used in scientific environments for laboratory monitoring and data collection, by schools for educational purposes, and by small and large business for data processing and computer graphics. When compared to mainframes, minicomputers are smaller, less expensive, less sensitive to the environment, and can be dedicated to a single task.

In the mid-1970s the minicomputer became very popular as a small-business computer. The lower-than-mainframe price and improved software made these cost effective for medium-sized (500 to 5,000 employees) businesses.

MICROCOMPUTERS

In the late 1970s the microcomputer emerged from its hobbyist status and shook the lower range of the minicomputer market. Microcomputers currently range in price from about $10,000 to $50,000. A microcomputer may have a single or complex multiple CPU design. The word size is usually 8 or 16 bits, with 64K to 512K of active memory. With larger memory, more sophisticated software programs and applications may be processed. Microcomputers are capable of supporting either single terminals or multiple terminals that simultaneously use the computer. A microcomputer may be capable of internal expansion and support multiple peripherals. The demarcation between micros and minis has rapidly diminished.

PERSONAL COMPUTERS

Another classification of computer size has established itself as a low-end microcomputer. This is the personal, or desk-top, computer, based on microcomputer technology. The personal computer is so named because it does one function, at one time, for one person. A personal computer is compact and is usually small enough to sit upon the surface of a desk.

Some personal computer peripherals are modular and may range from an R/F modulator, which allows the consumer to attach the unit to a television set, to memory expansion boards, which will triple the amount of active memory. Personal computers generally range from $500 to $15,000. A personal computer may operate independently or may communicate with a larger computer or data base (Dow Jones).

When used in a business environment, personal computers are actually "professional computers." For example, a professional writer may want a computer to do strictly word processing. A stockbroker or financial planner may want to perform spreadsheet functions and access the Dow Jones data base. A personal computer may do an excellent job of satisfying these needs while keeping the cost below $5,000.

Portable computers have been introduced that have the capabilities of personal or desk-top computers. Future personal computers will exceed the capabilities and power of today's microcomputers and so forth up the line.

A consumer should not be concerned with the exact definition of a type computer. Instead, the concern should be the needs and requirements. Once the business specifications have been established, the purchaser will be equipped to evaluate the different levels of computers.

SIZE VERSUS EFFICIENCY

At the present time the most efficient computers are in the $10,000 to $15,000 price range. For example, three $10,000 microcomputers can process more data faster than a $30,000 minicomputer. Twenty $30,000 minicomputers can process more data faster than a $600,000 mainframe. The $10,000 microcomputer will have more than double the capability and speed of a $5,000 personal computer.

The $10,000 microcomputer is about the most efficient, because of its simple design. It has sufficient processing size and complexity to utilize most of the important characteristics of electronic data processing, whereas a smaller computer does not effectively utilize the fixed- or base-cost components of a computer system. As computers become larger, they become more complex, because of the computers within the computers. These internal computers are more sophisticated and expensive than the simple microprocessor computer chips in a microcomputer. The sophisticated and complex design in larger computers is required for complex calculations, for interrelating large volumes of data from different sources and within different files, and for "directing traffic" within the computer system for many simultaneous users. Where these types of functions are not required, it is more efficient to use smaller computers.

A good rule of thumb is that a computer feature with twice the capability is four times as complex. For example, if computer *A* can sort and file 1000 data items in one minute, it will take four minutes to sort and file 2000 items. A computer that can sort and file 2000 items in one minute will be four times as complex as computer *A*.

The software for large computers is also more complex than the software for smaller computers. The ongoing personnel cost to maintain the software will increase at a greater rate than the original computer cost as the cost and size of the computer increases.

DISTRIBUTED DATA PROCESSING

Many businesses have taken advantage of the relative efficiency of smaller computers by separating information processing activities into multiple discrete subactivities. These subactivities can be efficiently performed by separate small computers. If there is limited interrelating and transferring of data, the small computers can efficiently communicate with each other. An example would be a chain of hotels. Each hotel would keep the necessary reservation information in its computer for every room within the hotel. A person could make a reservation at one hotel for another hotel, and the two computers would talk to each other. The computer at the hotel where the customer was making the reservation would print the information for the customer. The information would be stored in the computer at the "room-reserved" hotel.

The idea represented in the hotel example is called "distributed data processing." An interconnected chain of mini- or microcomputers may have unlimited capability. The machines may be connected to a "host" mainframe. The most inefficient aspect of distributed data processing is the communication between the computers. If the communication is constant or frequent, a large central computer will be more efficient than a network of small computers. This is the case where all users need access to an entire large file of information. An example is an airline schedule and reservation system.

6

SOURCES
OF COMPUTERS

The yellow pages of most major metropolitan areas contain numerous listings for computer vendors. Most businesses and other large organizations are continually bombarded by salespeople and literature from numerous types of computer organizations. In order to select the best vendor, it is usually most practical to select a vendor category or characteristic first. You should then have a manageable number of vendors to evaluate.

Prior to the 1970s and the minicomputers, nearly all computers were sold to the users directly by the manufacturers. They were sold either directly from the factory or from branch and district sales offices. With the advent of lower priced computers, the channels of distribution changed dramatically.

Vendor personnel support for software development, installation, training, and ongoing software maintenance are now extremely important. People who will be providing this service are much more important than the type of vendor or hardware brand.

There are several terms in the computer industry used to describe various computer vendors and their characteristics. The computer industry is completely unregulated. The term a vendor uses to describe itself may not have the same definition as the same term used in this text or by another vendor. A discussion of the terms commonly used to describe vendors follows.

MANUFACTURER-DIRECT

Buying directly from a manufacturer's factory provides the advantage of eliminating a third party and the third-party profit margin. Equipment maintenance can also be very good using this method. The manufacturer, however, usually provides little application software support. This software and the software support are much more important than the hardware, so this method of purchasing is not recommended except for very sophisticated users.

There are numerous manufacturers of small computers. Most of these are located in the major metropolitan high-technology areas. Sophisticated users in these areas may consider this source a viable alternative.

MANUFACTURER BRANCH OFFICE

Most of the major manufacturers such as IBM, Burroughs, and NCR sell their products through branch offices. These organizations' prices are not significantly lower than independent dealers, since they must include the cost of the branch sales office. Such vendors usually have limited application software, so that users must develop their own software or purchase from a third party. The organizations have high personnel turnover and move people up the organization or to different offices. Users, therefore, will often suffer from a lack of continuity of personnel support. Purchasing from this source should only be considered by users who have sophisticated data processing departments that do not require software personnel support from the computer vendor.

ORIGINAL EQUIPMENT MANUFACTURER (OEM)

The term *OEM* is used differently in the computer industry compared to most other industries. In most other industries the term is used to define the manufacturer of original or new equipment. Computer industry OEMs are generally assemblers of computer products manufactured by others.

The OEM concept in the computer industry proliferated in the late 1960s and early 1970s, when minicomputers became available to small business. The new companies that emerged at that time could build very cost-effective basic computer units, but did not have the resources or expertise to manufacture a full line of products and develop and sell cost-effective application software. The so-called OEMs purchased manufacturers' computers along with peripherals from other manufacturers and software from software houses and sold a complete cost-effective system to medium-sized businesses. OEM became the term for the independent seller of computer systems manufactured by others. The early computer industry OEMs often placed their label on the products they sold. Many of today's OEMs have the source manufacturer's label on the various component products of the system. Some OEMs provide excellent products and services, but, in general, the quality of these products and services varies considerably.

DISTRIBUTOR

A distributor purchases computer hardware peripherals and software packages in large quantities. He will generally sell a large variety of products from different manufacturers, using volume to obtain maximum discounts. Some distributors also provide hardware maintenance support, but they generally do not provide any software maintenance support. Distributors are a viable source of purchase, but only for users who do not require software maintenance support. Distributors sell primarily to dealers, not to end users.

SYSTEMS INTEGRATOR
(SYSTEMS HOUSE)

A systems integrator, or systems house, is a vendor who sells a variety of hardware and software products from various manufacturers to end users. This vendor may mix and match a variety of printers, terminals, computers, and software products to satisfy a wide range of consumer needs and configuration problems. The ideal systems integrator is able to offer a wide variety of solutions to a wide variety of problems. A systems integrator usually buys from a distributor, whereas an OEM, who carries a narrower range of products, buys directly from the various manufacturers of components.

COMPUTER DEALER

The term *computer dealer* is usually used to refer to a vendor who represents a narrower range of manufacturers' products than the systems integrator. These dealers may buy directly from the manufacturers or through a distributor.

Business computer dealers generally specialize in computers and sometimes in certain applications or certain industries. By contrast, many personal computer dealers sell noncomputer products or have a specialty retail computer store. Good business computer dealers use a direct sales force and have knowledgeable personnel to provide software and training support.

COMPUTER RETAIL STORE

Computer retail stores are usually considered to be those sales outlets that are located in a business area serving walk-in traffic. These organizations also utilize advertising to draw customers. This is in contrast to the previously mentioned dealers, systems integrators, and OEMs, which use a direct sales force. Computer retail stores, because of their high-rent locations and relatively high advertising and marketing costs, have less profit margin with which to fund software support service. Competition and volume in this segment of the industry may contribute to good prices for the consumer.

The retail-type outlet is probably the most effective source for low-price off-the-shelf computer products. The profitable selling of low-price products requires volume sales. The retail method is most effective for volume sales, and the American retail industry is the most effective ever in history.

There are now many excellent low-price computer products available to the business consumer, and the retail outlets are the natural source. There are many differences, however, between computer products and other traditional retail products. Computer products are tailored to the consumers' desires and needs and provide an ongoing service to the purchaser. The purchaser is often confused and lacks knowledge of how to select and use the products. Because of these factors, the computer retail outlet needs to provide more sophisticated service than other types of retail outlets.

Many computer stores have excellent training and service facilities, with knowledgeable sales and training personnel. These stores help develop and support user groups consisting of their customers. Many other computer stores, however, do not offer these facilities and services, attempting instead to obtain sales through splashy ads, price discounting, and brand-name promotion.

OFFICE PRODUCTS DEALER

Many office products dealers who have traditionally sold copiers, typewriters, and business supplies have now added small computers to their product line. Some of these dealers have developed good computer departments and are able to effectively lower their overhead and advertising costs by means of a wide range of products. Many dealers, however, do not have adequate and knowledgeable computer personnel.

DEPARTMENT STORE

Computers are now being sold through department stores. This is further exacerbating the problem of personal support from the selling organization.

Manufacturers are anxious to have their products exposed to consumers. They seem to be jumping at every channel of distribution, apparently receiving immediate benefits as their products fill the pipeline. They will suffer, however, in the future if the selling organization in contact with the end user does not provide adequate personal support.

USER GROUPS

Extensive personal support is an expensive aspect of business for a vendor. The cost of this support must be reflected in the price the user pays. If a user is buying the lowest priced product or enjoys paying for retail convenience and advertising rather than for personal support and service, the user will have to pay extra for support and/or spend more time learning and programming.

Some retail outlets do have knowledgeable people on the staff who can help the user. If their prices are to be competitive with other outlets that do not provide service, they must charge extra for the time of their quality people.

Another source of support for many users desiring a minimum initial cost is a "user group." A user group is a group of users who have common hardware, software, and application requirements. In user group meetings, the members share experiences and ideas and help each other. These can be extremely beneficial for the user, but the meetings will require an investment of time.

Many computer retail outlets are sponsoring or helping to establish user groups for their customers. A customer considering purchasing from a retail outlet should carefully evaluate the quality and extent of the vendor's training and software support. If these are minimal, but a low price warrants further consideration, then vendor-supported user groups should be evaluated.

TURNKEY VENDOR

We have left the turnkey vendor for last because this type of vendor is probably the most viable source for most business computer system purchasers. A turnkey vendor is a selling organization that sells hardware and software, tailors or customizes the software, tests the system with the user's data prior to delivery, and provides ongoing support and training for all aspects of the system. When the purchaser turns the key of a turnkey system, the system processes the purchaser's data.

Any of the previously mentioned sellers may be a turnkey vendor. However, a vendor's calling itself a turnkey vendor does not make it a turnkey vendor. Many cynics say, "Many self-called turnkey vendors sell a system, and when the purchaser turns the key, the vendor leaves."

Obviously, the best solution for most purchasers is a good turnkey system. This is because one vendor is responsible for both the hardware and software. The purchaser receives a complete system that works and full service for it. The price, however, must reflect the cost of doing business, and complete service does cost money. There are many tools and techniques available in the computer industry to reduce the cost of the services. The quality and cost of such services will vary considerably, according to the quality of the people behind them and the tools they use.

The greatest profit margin is in hardware, as against software and personal support. The purchaser will receive the greatest value if the people providing the software and personal support are receiving part of the hardware margin.

The adage "What you pay for is what you get" is only partially true in the computer industry. If you want complete systems and services, you must pay for them. If you do not pay, you do not have a chance. The only thing free is a sales pitch.

The cost of a complete functional system includes the cost of support and service, and also the costs of manufacturing, administration, advertising, sales staff, inventory, rent, and other items. Quality and efficiency in all areas vary considerably among the manufacturers and sellers in the computer industry. Consequently, prices for complete systems and support that are very similar vary considerably. Careful, informed, and intelligent shopping and evaluations will help you get the most for your money.

7

COMPUTER INDUSTRY TRENDS

The computer industry in 1982 was valued at $115 billion per year in the United States and is one of the fastest growing major industries in the U.S. and the world. Computers have dramatically increased in capability, with equally dramatic decreases in size and price. There are now affordable and cost-effective computers for nearly every small business and professional service.

The electronic computer industry and technology did not exist until after World War II. The first big electronic computer, built in 1946, filled a large room, contained 18,000 vacuum tubes, and used 140,000 watts of electricity. You can now get a more powerful computer than that original one on a two-dollar chip the size of a quarter that uses an insignificant amount of energy.

If the automobile industry had improved its technology at the same rate computer science has, you could buy a Mercedes-Benz for less than $40, it would get over 1,000 miles to the gallon of fuel, and it would go 100,000 miles without service.

Many experts are predicting a leveling off in price and standardization of products. I disagree and believe prices will continue to decline and the variety of products will increase. Everyone agrees that quality will continue to improve.

The most significant advances in small business computers have taken place during the last three years. Complete reliable computer systems have become available for less than $20,000, and they include tested software and integrated data handling and word processing.

These new computers require no data processing staff. They require much less operating personnel involvement than their predecessors required. If you have a computer system that is over three to five years old, you should consider replacement or major modifications to the system.

Current computer systems may be obsolete in three to five years, but a computer should pay for itself in one year. In addition, experience will put you in a better position to more effectively use the next generation of computers.

There are an estimated 12 million small businesses in the United States. This includes manufacturing, retail, distribution, attorneys, accountants, doctors, financial services, etc., with one to fifty employees. Less than 7 percent of these small businesses are currently utilizing computers or effectively using an outside computer service.

In the past, computers were sold primarily to large organizations. These organizations had, and could afford, competent, professional employees to operate the system, provide training, and develop or modify software. This segment (sales to the "sophisticated" users) of the business is currently 10 times the dollar volume of sales to the "unsophisticated" users. Both segments will continue to grow; however, the unsophisticated, small-business purchaser will represent the fastest growing segment. It is estimated that this segment of market purchasers will grow from $7 billion in sales in 1982 to $60 billion in sales in 1990.

The other fast-growing segment of purchasers of computers and computer services consists of people outside the data processing (DP) department of organizations that have such a department. The DP department within many organizations has become a bureaucratic structure with cumbersome procedures and lengthy delays for small projects. Many managers and professionals are finding it necessary to circumvent the DP department. They must do this in order to accomplish their cost-effective data processing projects at a low cost and on a timely basis. These managers and professionals are purchasing low-cost hardware, software, and services. They are writing their own programs, in DBMS, electronic spreadsheet, and word processing languages. It is estimated that this segment of market purchasers will grow from $12 billion in sales in 1982 to $88 billion in sales in 1990. (See Table 7–1 and Figs. 7–1 and 7–2.)

Table 7-1
UNITED STATES COMPUTER MARKET 1982 ACTUAL AND 1990 PROJECTED
(Billions of Dollars)

TYPE OF COMPUTER/SERVICE:	1982 $ VOLUME	1982 PERCENT OF TOTAL MARKET	1990 PROJECTED $ VOLUME	1990 PROJECTED MARKET PERCENT	1982–1990 ANNUAL COMPOUND GROWTH RATE	INCREASE (DECREASE) IN MARKET SHARE, PERCENT CHANGE
HARDWARE (Includes Peripherals and Media)						
Multiuser Mini- and Microcomputers:						
Small Business, Including Word Processing	$ 19	17%	$ 82	22%	20%	29%
Engineering and Manufacturing	6	5	18	5	15	0
Part of Mainframe Network	15	13	35	9	11	−31
Total Multiuser Mini/Micro	40	35	135	36	16	3
Mainframes	27	24	54	14	9	−42
Single-User Personal Computers	5	4	41	11	30	175
Total Hardware	72	63	230	61	16	−3
SOFTWARE AND SERVICES						
Outside Sales (Purchases)	12	10	97	25	30	150
In-House Software Development and Maintenance	31	27	53	14	7	−48
Total Software and Services	43	37	150	39	17	5
TOTAL	$115	100%	$380	100%	16%	0%

Table 7–1 (continued)
UNITED STATES COMPUTER MARKET 1982 ACTUAL AND 1990 PROJECTED
(Billions of Dollars)

TYPE OF PURCHASER	1982 $ VOLUME	1982 PERCENT OF TOTAL MARKET	1990 PROJECTED $ VOLUME	1990 PROJECTED MARKET PERCENT	1982–1990 ANNUAL COMPOUND GROWTH RATE	INCREASE (DECREASE) IN MARKET SHARE, PERCENT CHANGE
Large Organizations:						
DP-Department Controlled	$ 94	82%	$220	53%	11%	−29%
Non-DP-Department Controlled	12	10	88	23	28	130
Small Businesses, Organizations	7	6	60	16	31	167
Home	2	2	12	3	25	50
TOTAL	$115	100%	$380	100%	16%	0%

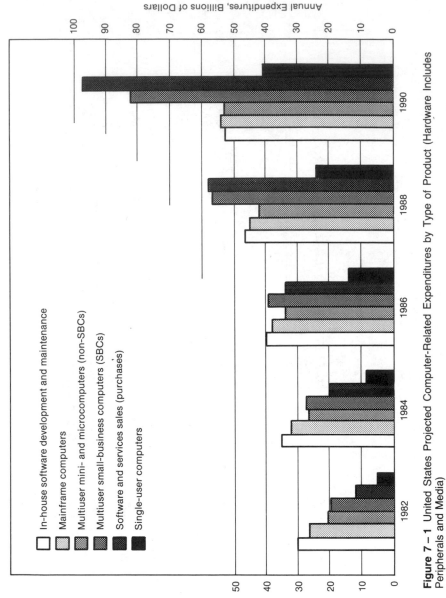

Figure 7 – 1 United States Projected Computer-Related Expenditures by Type of Product (Hardware Includes Peripherals and Media)

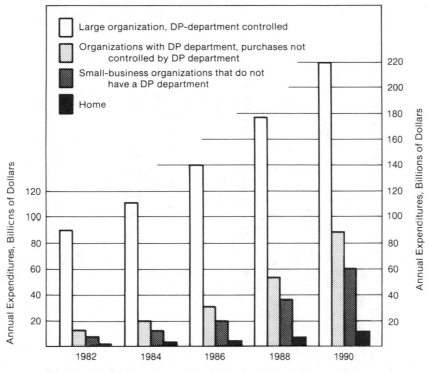

Figure 7 – 2 United States Projected Computer-Related Expenditures by Type of Purchaser

THE COMPANIES

In 1982, the 100 largest computer companies' DP sales in the United States totaled $80 billion. We estimate that the additional smaller companies' total sales are approximately $4 billion, bringing the industry total to $84 billion. (The estimated $31 billion that companies spend on internal data processing software development and maintenance brings the industry total sales and expenditures to $115 billion.)

Tables 7–2 and 7–3 and Fig. 7–3 are our estimated classifications of reported revenues into the categories we believe most useful to the current market. Breakdowns are somewhat difficult to estimate because there is no clear definition break between the various product categories. The chart in Fig. 7–3 displays the vigor that smaller companies are showing in the faster growing segments of the computer industry.

Table 7-2
1982 U.S. DATA PROCESSING REVENUES—LARGEST COMPUTER INDUSTRY COMPANIES
(Millions of Dollars)

| | 1982 SALES | HARDWARE, INCLUDING PERIPHERALS AND MEDIA | | | | | | SOFTWARE AND SERVICES |
| | | MAIN-FRAMES | MULTIUSER MINI- AND MICROCOMPUTERS | | | | |
			IN MAIN-FRAME NETWORKS	ENGINEERING AND MANU-FACTURING	SMALL BUSINESS AND WORD PROCESSING	SINGLE-USER PERSONAL	
IBM Corporation	$30,000	$18,000	$4,500	$1,500	$3,900	$600	$1,500
Percent IBM	100.0%	60.0%	15.0%	5.0%	13.0%	2.0%	5.0%
Percent Total	35.7%	68.0%	31.3%	23.7%	20.2%	11.4%	12.2%
2–10 Largest Companies	$24,350	$6,220	$5,610	$1,510	$8,494	$546	$1,970
Average	2,706	691	623	168	944	61	219
Percent 2–10	100.0%	25.5%	23.0%	6.2%	34.9%	2.2%	8.1%
Percent Total	29.0%	23.5%	39.0%	23.9%	44.1%	10.4%	16.0%
11–25 Largest Companies	$10,325	$1,410	$1,378	$356	$2,002	$1,803	$3,377
Average	688	94	92	24	133	120	225
Percent 11–25	100.0%	13.7%	13.3%	3.4%	19.4%	17.5%	32.7%
Percent Total	12.3%	5.3%	9.6%	5.6%	10.4%	34.3%	27.4%
26–50 Largest Companies	$8,026	$336	$1,833	$1,902	$2,226	$333	$1,396
Average	321	13	73	76	89	13	56
Percent 26–50	100.0%	4.2%	22.8%	23.7%	27.7%	4.1%	17.4%
Percent Total	9.6%	1.3%	12.8%	30.1%	11.5%	6.3%	11.3%

Table 7–2 (continued)
1982 U.S. DATA PROCESSING REVENUES—LARGEST COMPUTER INDUSTRY COMPANIES
(Millions of Dollars)

	1982 SALES	HARDWARE, INCLUDING PERIPHERALS AND MEDIA						SOFTWARE AND SERVICES
		MAIN-FRAMES	MULTIUSER MINI- AND MICROCCMPUTERS					
			IN MAIN-FRAME NETWORKS	ENGINEERING AND MANU-FACTURING	SMALL BUSINESS AND WORD PROCESSING	SINGLE-USER PERSONAL		
51–100 Largest Companies	$6,826	$363	$697	$608	$1,712	$938		$2,508
Average	137	7	14	12	34	19		50
Percent 51–100	100.0%	5.3%	10.2%	8.9%	25.1%	13.7%		36.7%
Percent Total	8.1%	1.4%	4.8%	9.6%	8.9%	17.9%		20.4%
All Others	$4,473	$134	$358	$447	$939	$1,029		$1,566
Percent All Others	100.0%	3.0%	8.0%	10.0%	21.0%	23.0%		35.0%
Percent Total	5.3%	0.5%	2.5%	7.1%	4.9%	19.6%		12.7%
Grand Total	$84,000	$26,463	$14,376	$6,323	$19,273	$5,249		$12,317
Percent Total	100.0%	31.5%	17.1%	7.5%	22.9%	6.2%		14.7%

Table 7–3
1982 U.S. DATA PROCESSING REVENUES—LARGEST COMPUTER INDUSTRY COMPANIES
(Millions of Dollars)

	1982 SALES RANK	1982 SALES	HARDWARE, INCLUDING PERIPHERALS AND MEDIA					SOFTWARE AND SERVICES
			MAIN-FRAMES	MULTIUSER MINI- AND MICROCOMPUTERS			SINGLE-USER PERSONAL	
				IN MAIN-FRAME NETWORKS	ENGINEERING AND MANU-FACTURING	SMALL BUSINESS AND WORD PROCESSING		
IBM Corporation	1	$30,000	$18,000	$4,500	$1,500	$3,900	$600	$1,500
DEC (Digital Equipment Corporation)	2	4,000		2,200	400	1,280	120	
Burroughs Corp. (Includes Memorex)	3	3,700	1,480	1,110		999	111	
Control Data Corp.	4	3,400	1,020	340	170	170		1,700
NCR Corporation	5	3,200	1,280	960		960		
Sperry Univac	6	3,100	1,240	930		930		
Hewlett-Packard	7	2,200			660	1,430	110	
Honeywell, Inc.	8	2,000	1,200			800		
Wang Laboratories	9	1,400		70	280	980	70	
Xerox Corporation	10	1,350				945	135	270
Storage Technology	11	1,300	910	195		195		
TRW, Inc.	12	850			85	85		680
General Electric	13	800				120		680
Data General Corp.	14	760		152		608		
Texas Instruments	15	750			75	638	38	
ITT Corporation	16	720		504		108		108
Apple Computer, Inc.	17	710					710	
Automatic Data Processing	18	700						700
Computer Sciences Corporation	19	660						660
Tandy Corporation (Radio Shack)	20	600					600	

#	Company							
21	Electronic Data Systems Corp.	560				11		549
22	Amdahl Corporation	500	500			49		
23	Motorola, Inc. (Including Codex & Four-Phase)	490		245	196			
24	Datapoint Corp.	470		282		188		
25	Commodore International	455					455	
26	Prime Computer, Inc.	450		90	135	225		
27	Comdisco, Inc.	430						430
28	McDonnell Douglas (Includes Microdata)	410				164		246
29	Rolm Corporation	400		160	240			
30	National Semiconductor	380	190	114		76		
31	Harris Corporation	375			300	75		
32	Mohawk Data Sciences (Includes Qantel)	370				296	74	
33	Computervision Corp.	365			365			
34	Management Assistance, Inc. (MAI, Basic 4)	360				234		126
35	Gould, Inc. (Includes SEL)	350		70	210	70		
36	Tymshare, Inc.	345						345
37	Tektronix, Inc.	335		84	168	84		
38	Tandem Computers	312		218		94		
39	Dataproducts Corp.	295		177		118	234	
40	Lanier Business Products	293				59		
41	Teletype Corporation	290		203		87		
42	Raytheon Data Systems	275		165		110		
43	Racal Corporation	270		108	81	81		
44	C. Itoh Electronics	255		51		204		
45	Northern Telecom	253		127		127		
46	Perkin-Elmer	251		25	176	50		
47	Boeing Computer Services	249						249
48	3M Corporation	245	98	74		49	25	
49	Paradyne Corporation	240	48	168		24		
50	Sanders Associates, Inc.	228			228			

Table 7–3 (continued)
1982 U.S. DATA PROCESSING REVENUES—LARGEST COMPUTER INDUSTRY COMPANIES
(Millions of Dollars)

	1982 SALES RANK	1982 SALES	HARDWARE, INCLUDING PERIPHERALS AND MEDIA					
				MULTIUSER MINI- AND MICROCOMPUTERS				
			MAIN-FRAMES	IN MAIN-FRAME NETWORKS	ENGINEERING AND MANU-FACTURING	SMALL BUSINESS AND WORD PROCESSING	SINGLE-USER PERSONAL	SOFTWARE AND SERVICES
M/A-Com, Inc. (Includes Ohio Scientific)	51	210				168	42	
Anacomp, Inc.	52	205						205
Philips Information	53	202				61	141	
Warner Communications (Atari)	54	200					200	
Signal Companies (Includes Ampex)	55	190	95	57		38		
Nixdorf Computer	56	185				185		
Wyly Corporation	57	182				55		127
CPT Corporation	58	180				54	126	
Allied Corp. (Includes Bunker Ramo)	59	177		177				
Informatics, Inc.	60	175						175
Telex Corporation	61	172	120	34	17			
Dun & Bradstreet (Includes NCSS)	62	169						169
General Instrument	63	160		48	80	32		
Shared Medical Systems	64	158						158
Bradford National	65	153						153
Pertec Computer Corp.	66	150		60		90		
Schlumberger, Ltd. (Includes Applicon)	67	149						149
Cray Research, Inc.	68	148	148					
United Telecom	69	147	15	15	74	15		44

Company							
Sun Information Services	70	145					145
Martin Marietta Corp.	71	142					142
Dysan Corporation	72	140	28		84	28	
Intergraph Corp.	73	138		138			
Tandon Corporation	74	135			68	68	
Gerber Scientific, Inc.	75	130		130			
Data Terminal Systems	76	127	38		89		
NEC (Subsidiary of Nippon Electric Corp.)	77	125			113	13	
Centronics Data Computer Corp.	78	123	37		86		
Mannesman-Tally	79	121	36		85		
Commerce Clearing House, Inc.	80	120					120
Quotron Systems, Inc.	81	119					119
Planning Research Corp.	82	118					118
Zenith Data Systems	83	117				117	
General Automation, Inc.	84	116		81	35		
Reynolds & Reynolds	85	115					115
National Data Corp.	86	114					114
ATV Jacquard	87	112			56	56	
Diebold, Inc.	88	111	111				
Modular Computer Systems, Inc.	89	110		88	22		
NBI, Inc.	90	109			87	22	
Televideo Systems, Inc.	91	105			74	32	
Management Science America, Inc.	92	100					100
Verbatim Corporation	93	98			49	49	
Interactive Data Corp (Subsidiary of Chase Manhattan)	94	96					96
Systems Industries	95	95	29		38	29	

Table 7–3 (continued)
1982 U.S. DATA PROCESSING REVENUES—LARGEST COMPUTER INDUSTRY COMPANIES
(Millions of Dollars)

	1982 SALES RANK	1982 SALES	HARDWARE, INCLUDING PERIPHERALS AND MEDIA						SOFTWARE AND SERVICES
			MAINFRAMES	MULTIUSER MINI- AND MICROCOMPUTERS			SINGLE-USER PERSONAL		
				IN MAINFRAME NETWORKS	ENGINEERING AND MANUFACTURING	SMALL BUSINESS AND WORD PROCESSING			
Lear Siegler, Inc.	96	90		27		63			
Triad Systems Corp.	97	89							89
American Express (First Data Resources)	98	87							87
Cado Systems Corp.	99	85				68	17		
Data Resources (Subsidiary of McGraw-Hill)	100	82							82
All Others		4,473	134	358	447	939	1,029		1,566
Grand Total		$84,000	$26,464	$14,376	$6,323	$19,273	$5,248		$12,316

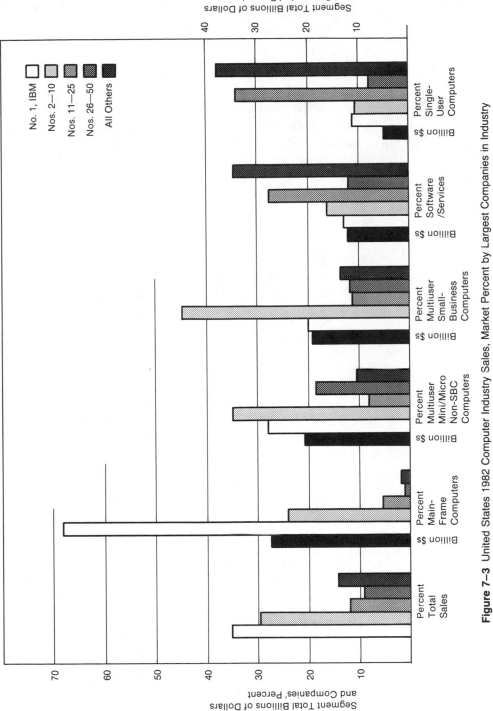

Figure 7–3 United States 1982 Computer Industry Sales, Market Percent by Largest Companies in Industry (Hardware includes peripherals and media)

TOTAL MARKET

IBM has an overwhelming domination of all segments of the computer industry. Its recent growth rate in sales, however, has not been as rapid as the industry's growth rate. IBM's sales represent 36 percent of the total computer market, more than those of the fifteen next largest companies put together. IBM's sales are 7.5 times that of the number two company, Digital Equipment Corporation (DEC).

A summary of the total computer industry's 1982 sales is as follows:

IBM	36%
Next 9 companies	29%
Next 15 companies	12%
Next 25 companies	10%
Next 50 companies	8%
Next 900 + companies	5%

The industry growth displays a trend of less domination by the large companies. For example, for the last several years IBM has been growing, but losing its market share nevertheless. (For the last four years IBM has shown steady growth, and its annual dollar *increases in sales* have exceeded the *total sales* of the number two company.) The estimated market share of the major companies over the last four years is as follows:

MARKET SHARE
PERCENT OF COMPUTER INDUSTRY SALES

	1979	1980	1981	1982
IBM	45%	40%	37%	36%
Top Ten Companies	80%	71%	67%	65%

The larger companies (1982 rank of 60 or higher) that have

shown substantial increases in the rankings since 1979 are as follows:

| COMPANY | PRIMARY PRODUCT | 1982 INDUSTRY SALES RANK | 1979 INDUSTRY SALES RANK | 1979 TO 1982 | |
				PERCENT SALES INCREASE	ANNUAL AVERAGE GROWTH RATE
DEC	Minicomputers	2	6	97%	25%
Wang	Minicomputers, Word Processors	9	14	242	50
ITT	Terminals, Printers	16	25	194	43
Apple	Personal Computers	17	70	1083	129
Tandy	Personal Computers	20	41	300	59
Commodore	Personal Computers	25	71	610	92
Prime	Minicomputers	26	38	194	43
Rolm	Minicomputers (Military)	28	93	981	121
Computervision	Minicomputers (Engineering)	33	52	254	52
Gould (SEL)	Minicomputers (Engineering)	35	62	393	70
Tandem	Minicomputers	38	66	373	68
Lanier	Word Processors	40	62	276	55
Paradyne	Modems	49	83	485	80
Philips	Word Processors	53	100	708	101
Warner (Atari)	Personal Computers	54	150	1900	171
CPT	Word Processors	58	84	291	58

Obviously, large annual percentage increases in sales are achieved with greater difficulty as the size of a company increases. DEC is the only company in the 1979 top ten whose growth rate has exceeded the industry average of 24 percent per year. All of the above-listed companies have been successful due to specialization.

Many of the fastest moving companies in the industry are outside the top 100. As the entry cost of getting into the computer industry goes down, these small companies break in by identifying and serving specialized niches in the industry.

MAINFRAMES

IBM is still very oriented towards the largest segment of the computer industry, the mainframe segment. Seventy-five percent of IBM's total revenues relate to its mainframe business (including peripherals and mini- and microcomputer communications associated with a host IBM mainframe). IBM's mainframe-related business approximated $22.5 billion in 1982. There are five other major mainframe companies. Each had $1 billion to $2 billion in annual sales in mainframes and related support equipment and services. These companies are Control Data, NCR, Burroughs, Sperry Univac, and Honeywell. They represent the computer establishment from the 1950s and 1960s. The top ten companies account for 92 percent of the mainframe segment's sales.

Several smaller American companies and some Japanese companies have developed what are called "plug-compatible mainframes," or PCMs. This segment of the industry received this name because a customer can unplug a large IBM mainframe and plug in a PCM, and all the IBM operating systems and software will run on the new system.

One of the more notable companies in this area is Amdahl Corporation (industry rank 22). Amdahl Corporation was founded in 1971 by Gene Amdahl, a former IBM senior executive. Amdahl Corporation's sales grew rapidly in the mid 1970s to $320 million in 1978. Since then, its growth rate has slowed; 1982 revenues were $500 million, reflecting "only" an 11 percent per year growth since 1978. Mr. Amdahl recently left Amdahl Corporation to form a new PCM company.

MINICOMPUTERS AND MICROCOMPUTERS

The next largest market segment of the computer industry is the technical and networking mini- and microcomputer segment. These minis and micros are used in networking, in conjunction with a mainframe, or in scientific and engineering applications. This segment represents approximately $21 billion in annual sales, with IBM and DEC accounting for approximately 40 percent of this total. The 50 largest companies in the computer industry account for approximately 90 percent of this segment's sales.

DEC, the number two computer company, has passed up all old-line computer companies except IBM, rising from a number four rank in 1980 and a number six rank in 1979. DEC has specialized in manufacturing minicomputers. The major companies in this market segment, with their estimated annual sales in this category, are as follows:

1. IBM $ 6.0 billion
2. DEC   2.6 billion
3. Burroughs   1.1 billion
4. NCR   1.0 billion
5. Sperry Univac   930 million
6. Hewlett-Packard   660 million

Another fast-rising major company in the computer industry is Wang. It became successful due to its approach of selling mini- and microcomputers for word processing and engineering applications within large organizations.

Prime and Tandem are companies that started in 1972 and 1974, respectively. They have grown rapidly, to become major forces in the minicomputer segment. They have successfully occupied the niche in the market that demands top quality, reliability, and performance in the $100,000 and higher price range computer systems.

Computervision, another rapidly growing company, started in 1969, specializing in minicomputers for computer automated design (CAD) for drafting and graphics. After several years of intensive research and development, sales grew to $70 million in 1978, doubled the next year, and doubled again over the next three years, to $365 million in 1982.

MULTIUSER SMALL-BUSINESS COMPUTERS AND WORD PROCESSORS

Multiuser small-business computers and word processors have been dominated by IBM, but are increasingly being influenced by companies outside of the top 50 in the industry. About 14 percent of this segment's sales is accounted for by companies smaller than the top 50. Larger and fast-rising companies in this segment attribute their success to specializing in niche markets that use smaller computers. Some of these companies are Data General, Texas Instruments, Basic Four, Wang, and Microdata. (We consider small-business computers and word processors as a single market segment, because it is becoming increasingly difficult to distinguish between the two types of computers, and in many cases the same computer is now used for both purposes.)

The leaders in multiuser small-business computers and word processing, with their estimated annual revenues in this category, are as follows:

1.	IBM	$ 3.9 billion
2.	Hewlett-Packard	1.4 billion
3.	DEC	1.3 billion
4.	Burroughs	1.0 billion
5.	Wang	980 million
6.	NCR	960 million
7.	Sperry Univac	930 million
8.	Texas Instruments	640 million
9.	Data General	600 million

Many companies in this area have a strong orientation towards word processing. These systems are used within large organizations separately from their mainframe systems.

Many of the rapidly rising companies sell systems used for general business accounting and management information and usually also include word processing capabilities. They usually sell to small and medium-sized businesses that do not have a data processing department. Because of these factors, seller software support and training are extremely important to the customer. Many of the sales are through independent, entrepreneurial dealers, most of which consider quality products and easy-to-use and support software more important than the manufacturer's volume-based advertising and sales strength.

Some smaller manufacturers appear to be doing a good job of giving the dealers what they want as compared to many of the major manufacturers' avoiding the use of independent dealers. Some of the rapidly growing small-business systems manufacturers outside the 100 largest industry companies are Alpha Micro, Altos, BTI, Durango, Dynabyte, Logical Machine Corp., Point 4, and Vector Graphics.

PERSONAL COMPUTERS

The smaller personal computer segment of the industry (including manufacturers of single-user word processors) is not dominated by the larger companies. Approximately 40 percent of this segment's sales come from companies smaller than the top 50.

The leaders in this segment, with their estimated annual revenues in this category, are as follows:

1.	Apple	$710 million
2.	IBM	600 million
2.	Tandy (Radio Shack)	600 million
4.	Commodore	455 million
5.	Lanier	230 million
6.	Atari	200 million

Most of the personal computers are sold through retail stores, although direct sales promoting professional use to large organizations is becoming a more common sales method.

SOFTWARE AND SERVICES

Software and services represents a large and rapidly growing segment of the market. This segment has been dominated by relatively large companies using mainframe computers to provide service bureau or timesharing services. An increasing influence, however, is coming from many of the smaller companies outside of the 100 industry giants. Rapidly growing products are packaged software, usually developed by small companies, and services being performed on smaller computers.

Some of the most significant recent advances in small-business computer systems have been in application software and programming aids. Many of these products are produced by small independent companies who sell their products to independent

turnkey system dealers. Most successful small systems are acquired on a "turnkey" purchase basis, where the hardware (physical equipment) and software are purchased together through a
single contract. The vendor tailors the software to the customer
and tests the system with the customer's data prior to delivery.
The computer is fully operational when it is delivered, and the
user merely "turns the key" for it to begin working.

PROLIFERATION OF COMPANIES

Along with (or perhaps the cause of) the rapid advances in computer systems' quality and reductions in price, there has been a
proliferation of computer hardware manufacturers and turnkey
vendors.

In the early 1970s, expensive, limited-capability computers
and electronic bookkeeping machines were sold to small businesses by major manufacturers such as IBM, Burroughs, and NCR,
through branch offices. They provided software packages for basic
bookkeeping activities such as accounts receivable, accounts payable, payroll, inventory, and general accounting.

As the market and applications expanded, these companies
continued their policies of selling through branch offices. The
applications software was centrally developed by people with
large-company backgrounds and often did not fulfill the smaller-
company needs. Many branch salespeople were not qualified, did
not understand the software, and overpromised the systems.

NCR and Burroughs have been rocked with numerous, well-
publicized lawsuits. IBM, with the muscle of its name and marketing dollars, has been able to sell numerous systems to small
businesses without promising much and by selling hardware
without the necessary software. As a result, IBM has many dis-
satisfied small business customers who are looking elsewhere and
giving negative referrals.

Many IBM customers became very disappointed when they
found that their small computer was only a personal computer
in capability (at a business computer price), and neither the computer nor its software were compatible with the next upward line
of IBM computers. Many of these (the 5100, 5110, and 5120 models)

were discontinued or made obsolete shortly after they were introduced.

The large number of suppliers is partially a result of IBM being the industry standard of comparison because of its large market share. Many small companies have been able to produce a better product, including software and software support, that is more closely attuned to the small- and medium-sized business market.

The large-size mainframe computer market continues to dominate the industry. These computers sell for millions of dollars each and are used by the very large organizations. The rate of growth in this segment, however, is declining. Because of this, and because of its size, this market is becoming increasingly competitive. It continues to receive the major portion of management attention of the major manufacturers.

SMALL-BUSINESS COMPUTER MARKET PROBLEMS AND OPPORTUNITIES

In the late 1970s many new small computer companies emerged to fill the small-customer void left by the major manufacturers. These companies' products have been sold primarily by independent dealers who are better attuned than the big-company branch salespeople to their small-business customers. Many of these dealers have developed their own software. In addition, many independent software firms have emerged. These sources resulted in much better hardware and software products and customer service than the big companies had provided.

The small-business computer market, however, has grown much faster than has the number of qualified people. Many of the businesses serving this market are undercapitalized.

Most of the small-business software packages are inadequate. Some look like the earlier large-company mainframe systems. Others are computer printouts of earlier small-business manual systems. Most packages effectively utilize the current hardware state-of-the-art technology from a processing or programming viewpoint, but do not effectively utilize the current technology from a management information and user viewpoint.

Much of the problem concerning the acceptability of computer systems within small businesses has been the lack of understandable and usable documentation (instructions) for the unsophisticated user. Most of the software has been developed by technically oriented people from large organizations with a lack of understanding of how small businesses actually work. In addition, the vendors have not adequately supported their customers with professional personnel who have a background in and/or understanding of business.

Many times, the major software problems relate to an overly complex design for small-business users and a lack of adequate user-oriented instructions. Most of the dealers lack the resources in capital and personnel to provide the necessary user training and "hand holding" during the implementation stages. Many times, no one on the computer dealer's staff really understands the software being sold.

The small-business requirements are diverse, and the large number of suppliers, products, and dealers has resulted in a rapid increase in the quality of products available for these numerous requirements. This fragmented source market, however, makes it very difficult for a customer to find the best products, suppliers, and support for his unique requirements.

In an effort to increase distribution, suppliers have resorted to utilizing retail outlets and office product and furniture dealers. Even IBM is resorting to this strategy, which, unfortunately, exacerbates the problem of lack of knowledgeable, personal support.

Because of the many problems in the small-business computer market and the shortcomings of the products, no sellers will guarantee their product. In fact, they will not even rent their products or provide trial service, demanding cash on delivery instead. Leases are actually high-rate financing, and the lending institutions always require other security.

The computer technology is far advanced, and if a seller had the right software products and support personnel, he could guarantee his products, rent them, or operate as a service bureau until the customer was satisfied. A good system and support would make the customer dependent upon the system and the supplier.

One of the major problems small businesses have in implementing a computer system is the initial loading of data (such as customers, vendors, products, codes, etc.) into the system and getting the basic software to work. The computer vendors sell the software systems, get paid, and leave the customer floundering to get the necessary data into the computer. (And, when the customer finally does get the data into the computer, he finds it does not do what he thought it would do.)

All these problems, in conjunction with the current trends in the various segments and the make-up of those segments, indicate a continued growth and opportunity for the smaller companies in the industry. Computers will continue to be increasingly used in a wider variety of and more specialized applications. They will be used more and more by less sophisticated customers. Specialized service and support to the users will be best provided by local companies, with the incentive for good service coming from the independent ownership environment.

Packaged software and programming aids will become an increasingly large and important product for the industry. The better products will continue to come from creative individuals working either on their own or in a small, creative group.

A summary and conclusions concerning the trends in the computer industry are as follows:

1. The number and variety of products are increasing.
2. Products are getting smaller and less expensive.
3. An increasingly larger number of computers and services are being purchased, used, and controlled by users rather than centralized data processing departments.
4. The fastest growing companies are those who specialize in a narrow range of products and services for a narrow range of customers.
5. Service companies and smaller computer companies represent the fastest growing companies.
6. The number of companies in the industry is increasing, and the most rapidly growing companies currently represent less than 50 percent of the industry's sales.
7. IBM will continue to grow but lose market share. For the foreseeable future, IBM will still be the dominant company in the industry.

USING COMPUTERS
FOR PROFIT

PART
TWO

8

PURCHASING A BUSINESS COMPUTER AND OTHER ALTERNATIVES

A business can use a computer cost effectively when there are three people in the office and the business needs to add one person (or more). A business needs three people in the administrative office. First there is the boss—the owner or manager. The boss needs an assistant and someone to answer the phone, etc. A third person is important for backup and relief. If the business is running smoothly with these three people, and management has all the information it needs on time, then a computer is probably not needed.

Current computers that cost about $600 per month, or less than one employee, are over *100 times as productive as any person* for many jobs. The computer does have many limitations, but it is most effective in performing repetitive tasks, putting the same information in many places, following instructions exactly, performing calculations, and transferring, sorting, and updating information.

Therefore, instead of adding the fourth person, it is better to add a computer, even if the computer is working only one hour per day. As utilization of the computer improves, it will keep the business from adding more people and will provide improved customer service and better decision-making information.

The primary indication that a computer will help a business is when profit margins, receivable collections, inventory, or purchasing efficiency is not up to expectations. When better and more timely information and analysis of these items will improve the business' return on investment, a computer will be a good investment. If the business management is asking its people to provide more information and analysis, and the people do not have enough time, a computer is needed for the business.

The three-people office should plan on spending about $15,000 to $20,000, or $600 to $800 per month, for its first computer. This will obtain a good one-input terminal and one-printer system that includes some customized or tailored application software (programs), sufficient capacity for business applications, and expansion capabilities.

The ratio of approximately $7,000 total cost or $300 per month per current office worker is a good starting guideline for larger businesses. This ratio is, of course, only a rough guideline and will vary according to the nature and complexity of the business.

Systems costing less than $10,000 are generally called "personal" computers and are not suitable for full business needs. They are called "personal" computers because they do only one thing at one time, cannot easily interrelate all the activities and data volumes that need to be interrelated in a business, and have very limited expansion capability. In addition, the vendors for personal computers generally provide only packaged software that cannot be altered, or else the user must do the programming. One of the advantages of a true business system is the program or software flexibility and vendor support.

The low-cost personal computers in business should more properly be called "professional computers." These computers provide an extremely useful low-cost tool for the professional who needs to analyze data or maintain and update documents that do not pertain to the voluminous accounting and detailed transaction records of the business.

A summary of the types of small computers used in business and when they should be used follows.

1. Home personal computer in business
   Price: $2,000 to $5,000 ($80 to $200 per month—3-year amortization, including interest, supplies and maintenance).
   Features: Two floppy disks, single user, light-use quality, no upward expansion, little software support from seller, off-the-shelf software.
   Who in business should buy: Professional with a lot of repetitive tasks and analysis, manipulation, and revision of small data files not interfaced with large central files.
   Justification: $80/month system operating 15 minutes per day needs to save a $20,000-per-year professional 15 minutes per day.
   Comments: Due to little vendor support, effective use will require extensive learning and possibly some user programming. A user should plan on 15 hours per week during initial 6 months' use for learning, programming, and participation in user groups. This may offset other savings, and the system, therefore, may not be cost justified.

2. Professional personal computer in business
   Price: $4,000 to $8,000 ($160 to $320 per month—3-year amortization, including interest, supplies and maintenance).
   Features: Two floppy disks, single user, commercial-grade quality, upward expansion capability, limited software support from seller, off-the-shelf software.
   Who in business should buy: Professional specialist with a lot of repetitive tasks and analysis, manipulation, and revision of data files not interfaced with large central files.
   Justification: $160/month system operating 30 minutes per day needs to save a $25,000-per-year professional 25 minutes per day (40 minutes for a $15,000 professional).
   Comments: Due to limited vendor support, effective use will require extensive learning and possibly some user high-level "programming." A user should plan on 15 hours per week during initial three months' use for learning and high-level "programming" (word processing, DBMS, or electronic spreadsheet development of master models). This may offset other savings, and the system, therefore, may not be cost justified.

3. Minimum small-business computer
   Price: $7,000 to $15,000 ($280 to $600 per month—3-year amortization, including interest, supplies and maintenance).
   Features: Two 1MB floppy disks or 5 to 10 MB hard disk, single user, expandable to multiuser and more disk, commercial grade, package with minimum customization software, some software and training support from vendor.
   Who should buy: Business with one person performing clerical,

typing, and posting activities six hours or more per day.

Justification: $280/month system used three hours per day should save one day per week outside help. In addition, the system should improve customer service and profit margins.

4. Small-business computer

Price: $15,000 to $30,000 ($600 to $1,200 per month—3-year amortization, including interest, supplies and maintenance).

Features: 10 to 30 MB hard disk, two or three users, expandable to more users and more disks, commercial grade, package and custom software, good software and training support from vendor.

Who should buy: Business with one full-time person performing clerical, typing and posting activities plus a secretary/receptionist, and the business needs to hire an additional person.

Justification: $480 to $1,000/month system used four hours per day should alleviate the need to hire an additional person. In addition, the system should improve customer service and profit margins.

A summary of typical prices for good, high-performance (speed) turnkey business computer systems follows in Table 8–1. This table reflects 1983 prices, with multipliers for later years footnoted. The prices represent actual installed systems obtained via competitive bids from quality turnkey vendors with successful track records for the respective configurations. Average installation time ranges from two days of self-instruction on the least expensive system listed to one year for the most expensive system. Systems installed by in-house DP departments generally cost double for the hardware and four times as much for software, including salaries for in-house programmers; in addition, installation time is usually two to four times longer.

The hardware prices listed represent commercial-grade equipment (except for the one-terminal, one-MB system) with expansion capability and downtime history less than 1 percent. Prices vary according to quality, processing speed, and features. For example, a Tandem system (one of the fastest growing companies—see Chapter 7), regarded as the Rolls-Royce of business computers, providing complete dual system operation and diagnostic computers within the computer, will have faster processing speeds and less than .01 percent downtime reliability, but can triple the hardware cost. Some name-brand systems, however, can double the cost with no increase in quality or perform-

Table 8-1
END USER BUDGET GUIDELINE FOR TURNKEY BUSINESS COMPUTER SYSTEMS*

NUMBER OF TERMINALS	ON-LINE DISK MB	END USER COST			PRINTERS	SOFTWARE DESCRIPTION
		HARDWARE	SOFTWARE	TOTAL	QUANTITY/DESCRIPTION	
1	1	$ 4,000	Included	$ 4,000	1/80 cps dot matrix or 15 cps letter-quality light use	off-the-shelf word processing and electronic spreadsheet, no training.
1	2	6,000	$ 1,000	7,000		
1	5	9,000	4,000	13,000	1/150 cps dot matrix or 40 cps letter-quality commercial grade (1*)	above plus off-the-shelf accounting packages, some training, some customization
2	10	15,000	6,000	21,000		
3	15	20,000	9,000	29,000		
4	20	26,000	13,000	39,000	2/2 of above (1*)	above plus some custom applications, more training
5	25	32,000	16,000	48,000		
6	30	36,000	18,000	54,000		
7	35	40,000	20,000	60,000		
8	40	44,000	22,000	66,000	3/3-(1*)	above plus specialized applications packages
9	50	46,000	24,000	70,000		
10	60	52,000	25,000	77,000	3/2-(1*) plus 1-300 lpm	above plus more extensive training
12	75	58,000	28,000	86,000		

Table 8–1 (continued)
END USER BUDGET GUIDELINE FOR TURNKEY BUSINESS COMPUTER SYSTEMS*

NUMBER OF TERMINALS	ON-LINE DISK MB	END USER COST			PRINTERS	
		HARDWARE	SOFTWARE	TOTAL	QUANTITY/DESCRIPTION	SOFTWARE DESCRIPTION
15	100	70,000	32,000	102,000	4/3-(1*) plus 1-300 lpm	above plus more complex packages
20	130	90,000	40,000	130,000		
25	170	110,000	45,000	155,000	5/4-(1*) plus 1-300 lpm	above plus extensive custom applications
30	200	130,000	50,000	180,000	6/5-(1*) plus 1-300 lpm	
40	300	170,000	60,000	230,000	7/5-(1*) plus 2-300 lpm	
50	400	210,000	70,000	280,000	8/6-(1*) plus 2-300 lpm	
75	700	310,000	90,000	400,000	9/7-(1*) plus 2-300 lpm	
100	1,000	400,000	100,000	500,000	10/8-(1*) plus 2-600 lpm	

*1983 prices. For years after 1983, for price, use 1983 prices times $.9^n$, for on-line disk MB, use 1983 on-line disk MB times 1.1^n, where n equals the number of years after 1983.

ance. Lower priced systems generally lack expansion capability and are slower, especially in a multiuser environment. The printer and on-line disk configurations are typical, but will vary according to specific application requirements.

Software requirements and costs also vary considerably according to specific application requirements. Descriptions relating to typical software costs are included in the table.

ALTERNATIVES TO PURCHASING

When a business decides to use modern electronic computer power to increase productivity, the business usually purchases a computer system. Alternatives to purchasing are leasing, timesharing, renting, and using service bureaus. Purchasing can be very beneficial, but the other alternatives may be more effective and contain less risks. Purchasing a computer system may expose you to additional add-on costs which are not disclosed in the initial agreement.

When you perform your vendor evaluation reference checks, make sure you ascertain the total price the vendor's customers paid in relation to the initially anticipated price. Some vendors will sell a base system, and when the customers commence operation, they find they need or should have additional items.

Supplies will be required for startup and will be an ongoing expense. Businesses typically spend about 1 percent per month of the total hardware cost for supplies. They usually initially require about four months' supplies costing about 4 percent of the total hardware cost.

Maintenance will also be an ongoing expense. Maintenance contracts usually require six months' to one year's prepayment of the contract amount. Hardware maintenance rates for a contract are usually also about 1 percent per month of the total hardware cost. Maintenance costs without a contract usually average about half the contract cost. The contract serves as an insurance policy, and service is usually better with a contract. With low-cost peripherals, many businesses have duplicate or multiple low-usage common peripherals. Downtime on one of these peripherals will not significantly hinder operations, so the business can eliminate maintenance contracts on these items cost effectively.

LEASING

Leasing of computer systems is generally just a method of financing them. It is often more expensive than direct purchase or installment financing. The leasing company generally requires security other than the computer system. It is not usually possible to stop lease payments and return the system. The lessee is obligated for the entire term of the lease.

If you are contemplating leasing a computer, you should carefully evaluate the terms and determine the entire obligation and cost exposure. This should then be compared with other financing alternatives.

Typical equivalent lease factors are shown in Table 8–2.

TIMESHARING

Timesharing is where users have terminals and connect, either directly or through a telephone line, to a central computer. The users share the central computer. Timesharing companies charge their users according to the connect time and central computer processing time. The central computers are usually powerful mainframes. A timesharing computer processes portions of each user's application using a consecutively interrupted technique. This interrupted processing (timesharing) is done so fast (in fractions of a second), that a user is not aware that the computer is being shared.

Many timesharing companies provide an extensive software library and access to substantial data bases. These companies also provide trained support personnel.

Timesharing unit costs have increased over the last ten years. Because of these increased costs and lower microcomputer costs, timesharing is not a viable alternative for most microcomputer or personal computer applications.

Timesharing is a viable alternative for professionals or businesses requiring limited computer usage for an application. This

Table 8–2
LEASE FACTOR EQUIVALENTS

MONTHLY PAYMENT, PERCENT TOTAL	ANNUAL PERCENTAGE RATE (APR) EQUIVALENT	
	$1 PURCHASE OPTION AT END	10% PURCHASE OPTION AT END
5 Years		
2.0%	7.4%	10.0%
2.1	9.5	12.0
2.2	11.5	13.8
2.3	13.5	15.5
2.4	15.4	17.3
2.5	17.3	19.1
2.6	19.1	20.8
2.7	20.9	22.5
2.8	22.7	24.2
2.9	24.4	25.8
3.0	26.1	27.4
3 Years		
3.1%	7.3%	12.2%
3.2	9.4	14.1
3.3	11.5	16.1
3.4	13.6	18.0
3.5	15.7	19.8
3.6	17.7	21.6
3.7	19.7	23.4
3.8	21.6	25.2
3.9	23.6	27.0
4.0	25.5	28.8
4.1	27.3	30.5

application should require extensive and complex computing power and/or access to the data bases provided by the timesharing company.

Some turnkey vendors offer timesharing service for software trial. This service may also be effective during the implementation phase, when usage is limited because not all systems have been developed or implemented. This type of service and implementation deserves serious consideration, since it enables the user to further evaluate the vendor while avoiding a large capital commitment.

SERVICE BUREAUS
AND COMPUTER SERVICES

A service bureau is a business with a computer for processing customers' data. The data are phoned or delivered to the service bureau, or the service bureau picks up the data from the customer.

Service bureau unit costs have been remaining stable over the last few years. The dramatic decreases in microcomputer costs have made microcomputers and personal computers more economical for most applications. Service bureaus are very effective for applications with extensive computing and printing requirements. These applications generally require government compliance and numerous data forms. Some cost-effective applications are payroll, income tax preparation, and medical records.

Before a business purchases a computer, it should have some of the standard activities performed on a computer by a computer service business. This will (1) minimize the cost exposure, (2) provide employee experience in preparing computer input, (3) provide employee experience in using computer reports, and (4) establish computer data bases for key information.

Payroll is the first activity that should be performed by a computer service bureau. If your business is manually preparing the payroll, either you are wasting money or your people do not have enough work to keep busy, and therefore, you do not need a computer.

A computer payroll service will be cost effective for a business that has three or more employees and pays its payroll clerk more than $4 per hour. A company named Paychex specializes in payrolls for businesses with less than fifty employees. A company named Pay-Fone is effective for businesses with more than twenty-five employees. Automatic Data Processing (ADP) and many banks are effective for larger employers. Many companies find a computer payroll service is so inexpensive and so effective, that they keep using the outside service after they get their own computer.

Table 8–3 presents a summary of the charges and features for Paychex and Pay-Fone.

The next computer service that should be utilized is one for the basic accounting activities. An accounting computer service

Table 8-3
COST FOR SEMIMONTHLY OR BIWEEKLY PAYROLL

	PAYCHEX		PAY-FONE	
NUMBER OF EMPLOYEES	MONTHLY COST	COST/ CHECK	MONTHLY COST	COST/ CHECK
1	17.00	8.50	45.78	22.89
3	17.00	2.84	47.34	7.89
10	37.00	1.85	52.80	2.64
25	55.00	1.10	64.50	1.29
50	80.00	.80	84.00	.84
	all-inclusive		plus $150 setup plus other charges	

Payroll services include:

	EMPLOYEE TIME TO DO MANUALLY (Average hours/month 2 payrolls)				
NUMBER OF EMPLOYEES	1	3	10	25	50
1. Computation of all deductions	1.0	1.5	3.5	5.5	8.0
2. Payroll checks with employee stubs	.7	1.0	2.0	3.5	5.0
3. Check register	.1	.2	.3	.5	.8
4. Departmental recap reports	—	—	.3	.5	.8
5. Quarterly state and federal tax reports	1.0	1.5	3.5	5.5	8.0
6. Annual W-2s	.1	.1	.1	.2	.3
	2.9	4.3	9.7	15.7	22.9
Computer cost to replace	$17	$17	$37	$55	$80
Hourly cost of employee to breakeven, $	5.86	3.95	3.81	3.50	3.49

will process checks or check stubs, deposits, and miscellaneous transactions to provide detailed records, analysis, and financial statements. The cost will vary with the number of transactions and the complexity of reporting. A general guideline for cost is about $100 per month per $50,000 per month sales, or 0.2 percent of sales. There are many computerized bookkeeping services, and many professional accountants provide this service. *Beware: There is a tremendous range of quality and cost in these services.*

The next items to computerize are accounts payable and

accounts receivable. When these activities are computerized, the business will have computerized customer and vendor data. If the business installs a computer system later, the data can be easily transferred to the in-house system. Many firms that provide the basic accounting services also provide payables and receivables services. When a computer service firm is selected, the range and quality of services should be carefully evaluated.

When a business is spending $400 or more per month on computer services, it should consider installing a computer system. The in-house system will provide additional labor savings, along with flexibility, custom features, and more timely information.

RENTING

Renting at a reasonable rate is not available for most of today's small computers. This is a sign of strong competition, rapid obsolescence, and vendor/customer problems. The market for used computer systems is very weak. Vendors cannot afford the exposure of renting when they have a high ratio of unsatisfied customers.

Vendors who provide complete, quality service find that renting is a powerful sales tool. Since it is expensive to change a computer system, satisfied customers become committed to their computer systems. The stop-rent exposure to these customers' vendors is, therefore, minimal.

Potential computer systems shoppers should seek renting or renting with purchase conversions as an alternative to direct purchase of the computer system. This alternative is not commonly available, but it should be seriously considered when it is available.

NOTHING DOWN AND FIRST YEAR FREE

Lease or installment financing and the new tax laws offer an opportunity, when properly used, to acquire a computer with nothing down. The first-year reduction in tax payments can be

Table 8–4
LEASE FINANCING COST
(APR = 20%, $10,000 Financed; Monthly Payment = $265)

	YEAR 0	YEAR 1	YEAR 2	YEAR 3	YEAR 4	YEAR 5	TOTAL
CASH PAYMENTS:							
Lease Payments	—	$3,179	$3,179	$3,179	$3,179	$3,179	$15,895
Maintenance	—	1,000	1,000	1,000	1,000	1,000	5,000
TOTAL	—	4,179	4,179	4,179	4,179	4,179	20,895
TAX DEDUCTIONS:							
Maintenance	—	1,000	1,000	1,000	1,000	1,000	5,000
Interest	—	1,885	1,602	1,255	834	319	5,895
Depreciation	1,500	2,200	2,100	2,100	2,100	—	10,000
TOTAL	1,500	5,085	4,702	4,355	3,934	1,319	20,895
Tax Reduction @ 50%	750	2,543	2,351	2,178	1,967	660	10,448
Investment Tax Credit	1,000	—	—	—	—	—	1,000
Total Cash Payments	—	4,179	4,179	4,179	4,179	4,179	20,895
Net Cost (Tax Reduction)	−1,750	1,637	1,828	2,002	2,212	3,520	9,448
Cost per Month	—	136	152	167	184	293	157
Cumulative Cost	$−1,750	$−114	$1,715	$3,716	$5,928	$9,448	$18,895

greater than the lease or installment payments and the maintenance contract charges.

If the software is purchased in conjunction with the hardware, the entire purchase may qualify for investment tax credit
and accelerated cost recovery (ACR) depreciation. A December
31 purchase will qualify for full benefits in the calendar year of
purchase. The investment tax credit is 10 percent of the purchase
price and is a direct reduction in taxes due to be paid. An immediate reduction in taxable income will be obtained from the
15 percent of cost depreciation permitted in the year of purchase;
this will further reduce taxes due to be paid by the effective
incremental tax rate. An additional 22 percent of cost depreciation is permitted in the following full calendar year. Moreover,
the interest and maintenance costs are tax deductible.

Computer systems often can be lease-financed for nothing
down, with all tax benefits going to the purchaser. In this case
the purchaser will actually be money ahead in the year of purchase, and the cumulative reduction in taxes through the following year will be greater than the financing and maintenance costs.

Professional tax counsel should be used when making any
major capital goods purchase.

Table 8–4 shows an example of a $10,000 purchase lease-
financed at a 20 percent annual interest rate.

9

JUSTIFICATION: THE FEASIBILITY STUDY

You may be asking yourself, "If I can buy a better computer system for less money in the future, why should I buy one now?" The answer is, if you don't need one, you shouldn't buy one. However, purchase of the right system, if you need it, can pay for itself in less than a year. Experience with a computer will put you in a better position to effectively utilize more powerful computers in the future. It is like going from a horse and buggy to learning to drive a car.

Many past purchasers do not regret their early expenditures and experiences, as these expenditures paid for themselves, and these purchasers are the ones that are most effectively utilizing the current products.

The computer industry's current annual sales are over $100 billion, and they have been growing at over 20 percent per year. Actual growth results have always exceeded authoritative projections. The current "official" projections for the industry are a 15 percent annual growth to over $150 billion in 1985 and over $350 billion in 1990.

The past and projected growth, due to declining prices, reflects a near doubling every year of installed computer power in the United States. Most of the growth in installed computer power has been due to expanded usage by existing users. Companies

that have used computers for many years are effectively expand-
ing the use of computers to more and more applications as their
own experience and computer performance relative to price
increase.

How will a computer pay for itself in one year? People costs
are going up, while electronic computer costs are going down.
For the things a computer does well, on a dollar basis, it is over
100 times as productive as people. For example, compared to a
person costing $1,200/month, an $800/month computer system
with its capabilities fully utilized, working 40 hours per week,
can produce over 100 times the data handling, filing, calculating,
and typing volumes.

You probably do not need 10 or 100 times the current work
produced. However, you have probably had situations where your
employees could not provide you the analysis or information you
requested because they were too busy or it would take too long.
You probably have had to do things yourself because your employees were too busy. With the right computer system, you will
be able to get a one-page summary report in one hour that would
take a person two weeks pulling files, tabulating, sorting, calculating, and summarizing to prepare.

The 100-plus-factor in productivity is also the reason for the
many computer "horror" stories we have all heard about. Can
you imagine the problems you would have if overnight you added
10 clerks, or 100 clerks, and did not properly select the new clerks,
instruct them, or train them?

If you use the same care in selecting a computer system or
computer service as you do in selecting a key person, and if you
manage the computer as carefully as you do a key person, you
should have minimal problems and can obtain substantial increases in productivity.

The one year or less payback most often comes from acquiring a computer in lieu of hiring people. This is especially true
in a growing business. In a stable business with high clerical costs,
a good computer system will reduce personnel costs. The greatest
profit improvements come when a business can utilize better
information to profitably reduce receivables or inventories, increase margins, or improve customer service. Profit-effective information is much more economically processed and generated
by a computer than by people.

Office automation equipment has dramatically increased in quality and capability, with equally dramatic decreases in price. The cost of good systems, however, may be more than $10,000 for equipment, plus more for personnel training and implementation. This is a significant amount for most offices, and it requires justification.

Office automation systems include data and word processing; document handling, reproduction, and filing; and communication. The equipment includes copiers, enlargers, reducers, computers, telephones, calculators, typing machines (from typewriters to word processors), filing equipment, recorders, and other audio-visual equipment.

A great deal has been written lately about productivity and the United States' slow or negative increase in productivity. Productivity does not necessarily mean producing the same amount of real goods or services in fewer hours; more often, it means producing more goods and services for each hour worked. Increased productivity can come from increased efficiency, but these increases are limited. The greatest increases come from the utilization of tools.

The greatest increases in productivity have been from our farms and factories. Our society has become more service oriented, yet the increases in productivity per office worker have been very low. Investment ratios show the reason why. The average investments in equipment and tools that a worker uses are now about $40,000 per farm worker and $25,000 per factory worker, but only $2,000 per office worker.

The equipment and tools for the farm and factory have been expensive but relatively easy to justify. Labor costs that relate directly to the product produced and sold are easy to measure and estimate before and after new equipment is implemented. The equipment has usually been proven and is ready to run when delivered. Increased productivity comes quickly.

How do you justify purchasing (or committing to long-term lease) office automation equipment? The purpose of the system obviously is to increase productivity. The increased productivity, therefore, must be enough to offset the cost of the system.

Many formal feasibility studies, budgets, and plans are exercises in futility since the results never match the projections. Most of the time detailed projections are out of date before the ink is dry. Many times the cost and effort involved in these exercises are not justified.

Most successful small businesses are successful because they do not have a planning bureaucracy. Because of this, they can react quickly to customer needs and the unpredictable changes in our dynamic economy.

Every successful business, however, does do some planning. This planning is often done on a somewhat informal but efficient method. This informal method should be recognized, maintained, and utilized in justifying productivity improvement investments.

This planning process takes place when the chief executive thinks about where the business is now and where it is going. He should ask questions such as:

> What is our product and service?
>
> How can these be better?
>
> How can we increase profits?
>
> What is the competition, and where is it going?
>
> What investments should we make?

Many times, the plan is not in writing; however, we recommend that some notes, even if only one page, be periodically maintained and filed. This will help solidify the thinking process and provide a reference for better planning in the future.

When investments are made, some financial projection is usually prepared. This may be concise and utilize percentages and ratios along with projected total monthly fixed costs.

Service-related businesses such as attorneys, accountants, employment agencies, etc., usually have little problem justifying office automation equipment, since office labor and related (square feet) expenses are the major expenses. For other businesses, the office expenses usually receive less attention from top management. Product productivity-related investments receive higher priority.

The business should view the office activities as a service center to the rest of the business. This service is the communication and information hub to make the total entity more productive. This information service center is vital in providing customer service and management information.

Inflation, high technology, high interest rates, and capital-intensive production, along with rapid changes in these same factors, have made timely, accurate, and usable management information increasingly important. Assets cost more and have an increasing exposure to loss or obsolescence. Good information systems have had a substantial impact in reducing inventories and receivables while also reducing losses of these items. Good information makes for better decisions concerning investments in capital equipment in all areas. Management information can result in better utilization of assets by improving the product or customer mix, pricing, or scheduling.

The basic methodology in justifying today's low-cost business computers is the same as that in justifying hiring additional office personnel. When office personnel are added, they may be necessary just for the organization to exist and keep up with necessary activities (such as mailing invoices) and regulations. Or, they may play a part in profit-enhancing items, such as improved customer service and pricing strategy analysis. All of these activities are things that a computer can do or assist with.

The basic justification for buying computers is in lieu of hiring people. A $50,000 system will cost about $2,000 per month or less than the cost of a person, including benefits, space, and other costs. In addition, there are tax advantages for equipment investment as compared to hiring people. Therefore, the basic justification for purchasing an expensive computer system is to replace one person or to avoid hiring one person who would be needed if the system were not purchased, per $50,000 investment. Any system costing less than $50,000 should be justified with improved service and analysis, improved employee morale, or alleviating work loads that would otherwise create increased personnel requirements in the future.

Most of the computer or office automation "horror stories" have been the result of a lack of proper planning. In ensuing chapters we will discuss the steps for implementing a successful business computer/word processing system. Office automation will involve some major changes in the way things are done, and success will require identification of and planning for these changes.

When business management personnel are evaluating the business's performance, contemplating improvements, and plan-

ning for the future, they should include the office's activities,
asking the following questions:

> What are the services produced by the office's activities?
>
> Should we improve these services?
>
> How much are the office costs, including salaries, benefits, floor
> space, etc.?
>
> Are these costs increasing?
>
> What are the alternatives?
>
> Where do we want to be in the future?
>
> Are there tools that will make us more effective in the future?
>
> Can we afford not to stay abreast of knowing how to utilize the
> current productivity tools?

Planning and justification of new ways of doing things, whether
done informally or formally, is a question-and-answer process.
Informal planning may be more effective for many smaller businesses. Some planning is important for success. Planned improvements in productivity, including improving the office, should be
justified as being an integral part of the total plan.

THE SUCCESSFUL SYSTEM AND WHAT TO BUY

PART THREE

10

ELEVEN STEPS TO SUCCESS

When it comes to purchasing and implementing a business computer system, many business manager purchasers do not use the same common sense and business principles that made them successful in general business management.

We have discussed software being the key to success in a business computer system. Software is the instructions or programs that tell the computer hardware (physical equipment) how to process and file your information and give you the reports you need to manage your business. Software is much more important than hardware in determining a computer installation's success. Vendors who are successful in installing software systems must select the right hardware for their software.

LIKE BUILDING A CUSTOM HOME

When acquiring a computer or making changes to your existing system, you should use your common sense and many of the same rules you would use in any comparably complex project. One of the best analogies is building a custom home.

The steps for a successful purchase follow.

1. SHOP AROUND. If you are contemplating a custom home, you will probably look at model homes to see if a standard home will satisfy your requirements and to obtain ideas and cost estimates. The same applies to building a custom computer system for your business.

Keep an open mind. You are not ready to prepare your requirements and seriously talk to computer salespeople or consultants until you have a good idea of the types of products available and their various features and capabilities. Do not trust anyone who is selling a product or service. Question the conflicting advice you hear.

2. SELECT A KEY MANAGER OR ADVISOR. Going back to the home analogy, if you decide you need a custom home, rather than a tract house, you probably want and need the services of a professional architect who specializes in your desired style of home. The architect must be a manager, not a carpenter.

The need for competent, professional computer advisors is no different. Make sure your advisors are: (1) independent; (2) people you feel comfortable with—the consultants should share your management philosophies and understand your business; (3) specialists with the skills and experience you need; and (4) managers, not just technicians. The individual is more important than the firm; make sure that the person you are talking to is a senior professional, and that you will not get merely a trainee after the job starts.

3. PREPARE YOUR REQUIREMENTS. Would you contract for a custom home without a blueprint, plans, and specifications?

It is very important to have your requirements prepared independently of any computer vendor. Vendors will try to sell you what they have and what is most profitable—not what you need.

You must have clear requirements concisely describing what you want your system to do, how and what information will be input, and the volumes.

These requirements pertain to software—not hardware! These preliminary requirements will be a guideline—like a floor plan drawing.

A consultant can professionally prepare your requirements.

These will be based on your needs and desires. A quality independent consultant will offer objective suggestions to help you obtain the best possible system at an optimum price.

If a builder (like a computer hardware vendor) prepares your plans, these plans will probably be designed to utilize the firm's existing plans, their experience in the type of houses they build, and the materials they have available. If they can, they will sell you the most profitable (usually expensive) materials even when something less expensive would perform as well.

4. Obtain Competitive Bids. Would you contract for a custom home without competitive bids?

Bids must be based on your previously prepared requirements. Competitive bids will save you considerable amounts, and you have a much greater chance of finding the best vendor and products for your unique requirements. Independent professional experience in this area will give you even greater leverage and access to the best potential vendors.

5. Visit Customers of Vendors with Best Responses. Would you select a home builder without looking at homes the firm has built?

It is easy for computer vendors to give good references, since many purchasers do not know they paid too much and received too little. Many purchasers do not want to admit (or find out) that they made a mistake. When you see an installation firsthand, you can see what the purchasers received for what they paid and how the vendor performed. An independent consultant can do preliminary professional screening and view the final demonstration with you.

6. have the Best Vendor Prepare Semidetailed Specifications and Schedule. The requirements you previously prepared were like a floor plan: approximate total square feet, a list of key desired features, and the lot plan. You now need a detailed blueprint for your house, together with final specifications of materials, colors, wiring, plumbing, etc.

For your business computer system, your preliminary requirements were a concise description of your information needs and volumes. You now need samples of final reports, input procedures, filing and record maintenance procedures, control features, and, finally, hardware features. We wait until now for this detail because a smooth-running system at an affordable price may be a compromise between your objectives and the selected vendor's capabilities and resources.

During this phase you will observe the vendor's personnel who will work with you and the quality of their initial work. A schedule will give you milestone management control and the basis for payments in relation to progress.

7. SIGN THE CONTRACT WITH NO MORE THAN 10 PERCENT DOWN. Would you sign a contract for a custom house and make a major payment without detailed plans and a schedule? Would you pay for work and materials before the services are performed and the materials delivered?

It is very important the previous steps be completed prior to making a down payment. The down payment should be minimal and should be all or partially (based on usable services performed) refundable.

Many computer systems vendors (like builders) are thinly capitalized. Beware of those who are asking their potential customers to provide their operating capital. Large vendors are just as dangerous, because the branch managers' or salespeople's bonuses and promotions are tied many times to signing orders and receiving the front money. In these cases, the vendors or salespeople are getting trapped in a financial cycle of needing to sign new orders rather than complete existing orders.

8. APPROVE THE VENDOR-PREPARED DETAIL SPECIFICATIONS AND TESTING PROCEDURES FOR ALL APPLICATIONS. This step represents the major part of the work in developing and implementing software programs. You must know how all the pieces fit together and interrelate.

You would not build your house one room at a time, relying only on hope that the separate carpenters will properly meet in the middle.

Since the specifications represent the major part of the work and expense in developing the software, we have separated them into three steps—numbers 3, 6, and 8, with each step containing more detail and refinement. This will continue through final testing and acceptance.

We are now at the stage of planning furniture and other interior details.

9. TEST YOUR DATA ON THE VENDOR'S EQUIPMENT. Would you accept your home and pay for it without checking to make sure that the plumbing and electricity work and the doors and windows open and close properly? Would you accept a car without test-driving it?

Software is "soft" in that it can be changed, just like the furniture can be rearranged. Structure, however, is very important: possible future changes must be anticipated and made as easily as possible. You will always want to make final adjustments. The final product will appear differently from what you envisioned during the design and planning.

It is important to have procedures for gathering test data and having the computer process and prepare information reports with this data. Training is a major consideration. Putting all your required data records into the computer will also require a major effort. Training, testing, and building data files can be combined and done on the vendor's computer prior to delivery of your computer. In order to minimize your exposure, the first application tested and installed should be the most complex.

10. TAKE DELIVERY OF EQUIPMENT—THE FIRST MAJOR PAYMENT WILL BE AFTER THE SYSTEM IS RUNNING AND PRODUCING TO YOUR SATISFACTION. Your best method for controlling your computer purchase is with your checkbook. When you build a house, you make progress payments as work is completed. You also withhold a retention. A retention prevents the builder from receiving all the profit during the initial stages. The retention provides incentive for the builder to properly and expeditiously complete the project.

A computer project is no different. Progress payments will probably be required, but these should be for value received. The major expense is the hardware, and it should be paid for (except for a security or good-faith deposit) when received. The vendor should not receive all the profit until after the project is complete.

11. INSTALL ALL APPLICATIONS—MAKE FINAL PAYMENT ONLY WHEN COMPLETE. Installing and learning to use a complete system will take effort and time. It will require a change in some of your methods of operation. Your employees' jobs will be easier and more productive, but different.

Because of these factors, you cannot immediately install all applications. The vendor will need to support you, train your employees, and modify the software until completion of the entire project.

It would be like building a large house with a plan for building the central portion and residence bedrooms first. The guest wings, game rooms, etc., are to be built and phased in later, after you move in to the part completed in the first phase. Payments, of course, will be made as work is completed.

COMMON SENSE

We have avoided the use of terms unique to the computer world. You do not need to learn a new, extensive vocabulary. You do not need to know how a computer works. If you are building a new electronic home, you do not need to know how the electronic appliances and devices work.

Whether buying a business computer system or building a home, you must know what you want. You must use your common sense, project management controls, and payments in relation to completion to make sure you receive what you want.

SMALL SYSTEM LIKE A TRACT HOUSE

Buying many of today's low-cost computers with off-the-shelf packaged software is like buying a tract house. When you complete the "shop around" step in our success method, you may feel you can be comfortable and happy in a tract home. Similarly, after shopping around, you may feel that a personal professional computer and off-the-shelf packaged software will satisfy your computer needs.

In both cases you eliminate many of the steps involved in acquiring a customized product. You will not require an architect, but an advisor may be helpful in the initial stages. You will see the finished product and be buying it upon completion. You should, however, carefully inspect and test the products. You will probably accept the seller's standard terms and make a single payment.

There are many choices available for both tract houses and off-the-shelf computer systems. Prices vary considerably in both cases due to quality and features. With computers, you need to judge the commercial grade and expected service and performance. Location has a considerable effect on home prices. Vendor margins, along with efficiency, overhead, advertising, and selling costs will have a similar effect on computer prices. You should judge what the price reflects and whether it is worth it to you.

Even with a tract house, you end up with a custom product when you add the interior and landscaping final touches and insert your furniture. Similarly, you will tailor your computer software to yourself when you insert the system parameters and your data. You want both finished products to suit your personal life or business style.

The steps in the eleven-step success method that are applicable to the inexpensive off-the-shelf systems are: (1) shop around, (3) prepare your requirements, (4) obtain competitive bids (or prices with features), (5) visit customers of vendors with best responses, and (9) test your data on the vendor's equipment.

Obtaining the optimum product requires diligent shopping. As with custom products, you must know what you want, i.e., have predefined requirements. You must be able to visualize how your home shell will look when completely furnished. You must be able to visualize how your job or business will operate when the computer system is implemented. In both cases, careful and knowledgeable shopping are the keys to success.

11

PREPARING REQUIREMENTS AND REQUESTS FOR PROPOSALS

One of the key factors in obtaining an optimum and cost-effective computer system is knowing what you want the computer system to do. You must specify these requirements, and you need to obtain competitive proposals to satisfy them. The extent and detail of the requirements will increase as the size and custom or tailored features of the computer system increase. In all cases you should list what you want the system to accomplish. The basic requirements are always for the software first, which, when selected, will determine the hardware requirements.

OFF-THE-SHELF SYSTEMS

The requirements for off-the-shelf software should include the types of projects the software will be used for. The primary software packages in this category are word processing, electronic spreadsheets, and data base management. An example for word processing requirements is shown in Fig. 11–1.

In the figure, the prospective purchaser has first listed the proposed uses of the system. After preliminary shopping to become familiar with the capabilities of various word processing systems, the buyer is able to list the desired features that are

PRIMARY USES:

1. Standard forms - leases, wills, trusts, etc. (average of 70 documents on file, average of 20 pages [up to 60] each)
2. Changes, corrections to standard forms (2 documents per day)
3. Letters, reports, etc. (10 per day)
4. Mail list (2000 names; 100 additions, 100 changes, 50 deletions per month)

DESIRED FEATURES:

1. All standard text editing features
2. Automatic merge with mail list
3. Spelling checking capability
4. Simultaneous, independent print/edit operations
5. Automatic word wrap
6. Automatic document indexing and formatting
7. Direct forward/reverse document/page access
8. Automatic line centering and flush right
9. Automatic displayed underscore
10. Automatic hyphenation and justification
11. Automatic document reformatting and pagination, with widow and orphan line protect
12. Automatic indenting
13. Global search and replace
14. Save/recall holding memories
15. Automatic letter writing
16. Variable vertical spacing
17. Super- and subscripts
18. Document and selected text assembly
19. Automatic headers and footers
20. Automatic page numbering
21. Columnar capability
22. Arithmetic capability
23. Forms capability
24. Sort and select capability
25. Key phrase and update

FIGURE 11-1 Sample Word Processing System Requirements

important. The buyer will now be able to ask the potential vendors questions or have them complete this checklist, although he may prefer to test systems while completing the checklist himself.

SMALL-BUSINESS COMPUTERS

A small-business computer system costing less than $20,000 for hardware and software will probably use packaged software with some tailoring. The $20,000 system will probably include two terminals, a printer, and a hard disk. In this situation, and for larger systems, it is best to list the standard applications desired and the relative volumes of use of each. A form for doing this is shown in Fig. 11–2. Factors for estimating the disk requirements are included. The actual factors for the disk requirements will vary considerably based upon the amount of related information maintained for each activity and the sophistication or complexity of the system design. Vendors' hardware and software will differ in their impact on disk requirements due to the difference in their system overhead requirements. Because of all these factors, any preliminary disk requirement estimate may be substantially revised after the vendor is selected.

COMPLEX BUSINESS SYSTEMS

More complex business applications, including basic accounting, will require more extensive and customized requirements. Such requirements must be in writing. They should be clear and concise. The purpose of the written requirements and request for proposal is to help the potential vendors understand what you want their system and personnel to do. You want to make it easy for vendors to respond.

The request for proposals should provide for a flexible response format. Requests for a rigid checklist, detailed vendor data, and detailed hardware specifications will discourage responses, and many times the requested information is not important. The initial vendors' replies in their individual styles will provide insights as to the quality of their work.

SYSTEM/ FILE OR ACTIVITY	(A) COMPUTER- PRINTED?	(B) VOLUME	(C) VOLUME/ FRE- QUENCY	(D) DISK, KB FACTOR	(E) (B) × (D) DISK, KB
1. ORDER ENTRY					
a. Sales Orders	[ ]	_____	/mo	.2	_____
b. Order Items		_____	/mo	.1	_____
c. Open Orders		_____	Avg.	1.0	_____
2. SALES REVENUES					
a. Customers		_____	Tot	1.0	_____
b. Invoices	[ ]	_____	/mo	.1	_____
c. Invoice Items		_____	/mo	.1	_____
3. ACCOUNTS RECEIVABLE					
a. Balance Forward [ ]					
or Open Item [ ]					
b. Monthly Statements	[ ]	_____	/mo	1.0	_____
c. Open Items		_____	Avg	.3	_____
d. Checks or Cash Received		_____	/mo	.1	_____
4. INVENTORY					
a. Number of Products		_____	Tot	1.0	_____
5. PURCHASING					
a. Purchase Orders	[ ]	_____	/mo	.2	_____
b. P.O. Items		_____	/mo	.1	_____
c. Open P.O.s		_____	Avg	1.0	_____
6. ACCOUNTS PAYABLE					
a. Vendors		_____	Tot	.7	_____
b. Invoices Received		_____	/mo	.1	_____
c. Invoice or General Ledger Account Items		_____	/mo	.05	_____
d. Unpaid Invoices		_____	Avg	.1	_____
e. Checks Issued	[ ]	_____	/mo	.1	_____
7. JOB COST					
a. Charge Codes		_____	Tot	.1	_____
b. Charges (Items)		_____	/mo	.05	_____
8. PAYROLL					
a. Employees		_____	Avg	1.0	_____
b. Employees—W–2s		_____	Tot	.5	_____
c. Paychecks	[ ]	_____	/mo	.3	_____

FIGURE 11-2 Computer System Estimating Worksheet

SYSTEM/ FILE OR ACTIVITY	(A) COMPUTER- PRINTED?	(B) VOLUME	(C) VOLUME/ FRE- QUENCY	(D) DISK, KB FACTOR	(E) (B) × (D) DISK, KB
9. FIXED ASSETS					
a. Total Items		_____	Tot	.7	_____
b. Maintenance Items		_____	Tot	.4	_____
c. Maintenance Charges		_____	/mo	.05	_____
10. GENERAL LEDGER					
a. Number of Accounts		_____	Tot	1.0	_____
b. Journal Line Items		_____	/mo	1.0	_____
11. WORD PROCESSING					
a. Text Pages		_____	/mo	3.0	_____
b. Largest Documents, Pages		_____	Tot	3.0	_____
c. Mail List, Number		_____	Tot	.2	_____
12. ELECTRONIC SPREADSHEET					
a. Pages		_____	/mo	3.0	_____
13. GRAPHICS					
a. Pages		_____	/mo	3.0	_____
14. DATA BASE MANAGEMENT SYSTEMS					
a. Master File Items		_____	Tot	1.0	_____
b. Open Transactions		_____	Tot	.2	_____
15. OTHER		_____			_____
		_____			_____
16. TOTAL, KB Disk Requirement					_____
TOTAL, MB Disk Requirement (KB ÷ 1000)					_____

Tot = Total number on-line, Avg = average number on-line, /mo = number of items or transactions per month. KB = 1000 characters (1000 K = 1 megabyte (MB)).

FIGURE 11-2 (continued) Computer System Estimating Worksheet

A CASE STUDY

A sample request for proposals and some of the requirement pages are shown in Figs. 11–3 through 11–8. The example is for a hospital, since it is assumed that most readers have had some experience, either as a visitor or patient, in seeing a hospital in operation. Hospitals represent a major business industry and have many business problems common to all businesses. They also have some unique problems and requirements.

The first page (Fig. 11–3) of the request for proposal should state the reply requirements. These should be kept simple. You should state the dates and basic information that you desire.

You should provide an overview of the business, the current situation, and basic objectives (Fig. 11–4).

The next step is to identify the major functional areas, and then the applications within each area. This is analogous to developing room requirements for your home. In the example, the hospital, currently using a service bureau, has listed the systems and included a graded (Λ to F, or do not have and need) rating of the current systems. The hospital, of course, would like all applications to be functioning with an A or B grade. This grade analysis is not necessary, but it is helpful for a prospective computer vendor in evaluating the hospital's needs and potential improvements. It is also helpful for potential vendors for getting to know the customer.

The number of printers and CRTs to quote should be stated (Fig. 11–4). These numbers may change, but will provide a common basis for comparison with initial price estimates. It is not necessary to specify the computer size (CPU memory K) or disk storage (MB). These requirements will vary according to vendors' hardware and software features; each vendor will propose what is appropriate for his envisaged solution.

Key volumes (Fig. 11–5) should be included. This will further help to outline the application requirements.

The key item in the system requirements is the application software requirements. You need to specify what information needs to be filed and available for inquiry and reports. You need to specify what reports on this information you will need. You need to show how the information interrelates.

A flowchart (Fig. 11–6) is extremely helpful, serving as a one-page table of contents to all files and reports. This is analogous to making a floor plan for your home. You may use any flowchart symbols or procedures that are useful to you and easily understandable by others. We have selected three symbols: one for files of information, one for reports, and one for input activity. The

REQUEST FOR PROPOSAL
COMMUNITY HOSPITAL

A preliminary system description and requirements are attached. We are requesting PRELIMINARY PROPOSALS AND ESTIMATES FOR A TURNKEY SYSTEM based on the attached requirements.

General file contents and input and output descriptions are included. These items are abbreviated, preliminary, subject to modification, and intended only as guidelines for interrelations of proposed input/output. Alternatives will be considered. Standard items, edit and balance reports, registers, etc., that are normal and included in most systems have been omitted from these descriptions. Final detail specifications will be prepared by the vendor and approved by us.

A PRELIMINARY PROPOSAL AND ESTIMATE SHOULD INCLUDE: hardware descriptions, software descriptions, cost per item, cost for detail specifications, timing of payments, and estimated time to completion. We are seeking an *October 1, 198X installation.*

Please use the attached RFP Evaluation Form [Figure 11–6, with example and instructions shown as Figures 11–7 and 11–8, respectively] or provide the data requested.

You should indicate requirements in this request that may be a problem. You may propose alternatives or indicate the cost of providing specific requirements.

The quality (brevity is a plus) of the proposal will help us determine which vendor(s) will meet with the client to refine their proposal and estimate.

After a vendor is selected, the next phase will be preparation of detailed specifications by the vendor. These specifications will include report layouts, input formats and requirements, system features, file layouts, and processing logic. The final contract amount based on final specifications will be subject to modification from a preliminary proposal that will be based on the enclosed specifications.

We would like to *receive all responses by July 30, 198X.*

Please call if you have any questions or would like additional clarification on any item.

FIGURE 11–3 Sample Request For Proposal Cover Letter

flowchart will show how information goes into the computer files and from what files each report obtains its information. This flowchart serves as a useful checklist to assure that some key information item or key activity has not been omitted.

COMMUNITY HOSPITAL
SYSTEM REQUIREMENTS

OVERVIEW

We are a 200-bed hospital. We are seeking a turnkey hardware and software computer system or on-line service to replace a time-sharing service. The approximate budget is $250,000 or less.

The hospital industry has many specialized requirements due to Medicare/Medi-Cal, other insurance company requirements, specialized personnel, and 24-hour, no-holiday operation. The software system vendor, therefore, must have knowledge and experience in this industry.

The current time-sharing system was installed four years ago. It consists of a dual key-to-diskette data station and an on-line transmitting, receiving, and printing terminal (no VDT display).

The configuration limits the current system flexibility, and we would like on-line interactive capability.

The status of the current systems and the desired systems are as follows:

	A	B	C	D	F	N
Medical Staff and Patient Administration				X		
On-line admitting						X
Patient charges			X			
Patient bills		X				
Insurance forms		X				
Medical staff reports						X
Charge/nurse statistics					X	
Accounts Receivable		X				
Accounts Payable/Inventory					X	
Open purchase orders						X
Accounts payable			X			
Inventory						X
Payroll/Personnel			X			
Payroll			X			
Personnel			X			
Fixed Assets						X
General Ledger				X		

A through F = have on existing system; A = working very well; F = working very poorly; N = do not have, but would like.

FIGURE 11–4 Sample System Requirements Overview

**COMMUNITY HOSPITAL
SYSTEM REQUIREMENTS**

OVERVIEW (continued)

The hospital executives and committees have many requirements for special reports. The system should have a data base management system (DBMS) with ad hoc reporting capability. These reports could come from the hospital administration transaction data. In addition, the system should have the capability for the hospital personnel to create their own special data bases (e.g., outside contracts) and reports from these data bases.

The attached software requirements represent an overview of the business and volumes and reflect a "wish list" of the information desired. However, these requirements are somewhat simplified, and additional complexities are anticipated to be highlighted when the detailed specifications are prepared.

These requirements are flexible. Some customization of packages will probably be expected. A desired feature of the software will be its flexibility and ease of modification. The package and custom software must be maintained by the vendor, as the hospital does not want to have a data processing staff.

The initial hardware requirements that should be quoted are:

	CRTs	PRINTERS
Inpatient admitting	2	1 (c)
Outpatient admitting	1	1 (c)
Emergency room	1	
Patient charges, billing, cash receipts, insurance	2	1 (1)
Inventory and purchasing	1	1 (c)
Medical records	1	
Payroll/personnel	1	
Accounts payable and general accounting	2	1 (1)
Nursing stations	3	
Total	14	5

(c) = 9″ width, character, dot matrix
(1) = line printer (dot matrix acceptable)

FIGURE 11–4 (continued) Sample System Requirements Overview

COMMUNITY HOSPITAL
SYSTEM REQUIREMENTS

OVERVIEW (continued)

This hardware and software system will probably be phased in over a one-year period. In addition to an estimated cost for the complete system, we would like a cost estimate for the initial installation. The initial installation should replace the existing software systems on time sharing and should reflect approximately half the above number of CRTs and printers.

The system must be expandable, as the hospital may be doubling the number of beds in the near future. The system must have the capability of adding more terminals for inquiry or input. All printers should be "system" printers working from a spool.

The following sections indicate general requirements for master files (excludes company codes and transaction, history and system update files), system inputs (excludes master file updates) and output reports (excludes edit and balance and normal control registers).

FIGURE 11-4 (continued) Sample System Requirements Overview

Lists of the key items to be included on the various reports or in the various files should follow the flowchart (Fig. 11–7; the complete lists are not necessary for this example and are not included in this book). These lists should include only the items that you feel are unique or that the vendors may not have in their standard packages. It is not necessary to include detail and report layouts. The vendors can more efficiently do this utilizing their computer software programs.

These finished requirements should provide you useful documentation of your business information processing activities and needs. This will be helpful for better understanding your business even if you do not computerize. If you do computerize, your written plan and objectives will help you be successful in obtaining an effectively working system. If you do not know where you are going, you have no chance of getting there!

It is most helpful to have a standard format for tabulating

COMMUNITY HOSPITAL
SYSTEM REQUIREMENTS

ESTIMATED KEY VOLUMES

Medical Staff and Patient Administration
Beds	200
Occupancy (average)	60%
Patients' file	10,000 + 2,220/month
Inpatients	2,100/month
Outpatients	800/month
Emergency room	1,000/month
Medical staff	350
Pharmacy items	6,000
Other charge items	3,000

Accounts Receivable
Accounts open for charge	1,000
Patient charges	2,500/day
Accounts receivable, open accounts	13,000
Cash receipts	6,000/month

Accounts Payable/Inventory
Vendors	600
Inventory charge items	6,000
Inventory nonpatient-charge items	3,000
Purchase orders total	1,000/month
Purchase order items	10,000/month
Accounts payable open invoices	2,000
Vendor invoices	1,300/month
Vendor checks	400/month

Payroll/Personnel   500 current
Employees	900 W-2's

Fixed assets
Fixed assets	9,000
Maintenance items	500
Maintenance charges	1,000

General Ledger
General ledger accounts (including subaccounts)	3,500
Journal entry line items	12,000/month

FIGURE 11–5 Sample System Requirements Volumes

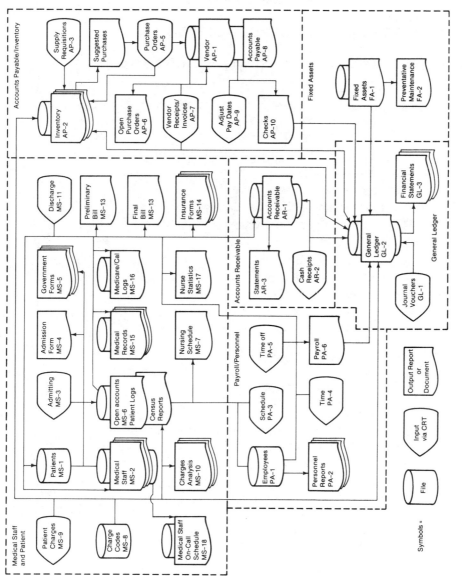

FIGURE 11-6 Sample System Flowchart

155

COMMUNITY HOSPITAL
SYSTEM REQUIREMENTS

MEDICAL STAFF AND PATIENT ADMINISTRATION

MS–1 (I,F)* Patient file (10,000, growing by 2,200 per month)

1. Number
2–40. Name, address, etc.; normal information, including insurance, for admission form
41. Date first entered
42. Original doctor (medical staff) number
43. Date last activity
44. Last activity code
45. Last activity discharge diagnosis
46. Number of inpatient visits
47. Number of outpatient visits
48. Doctor's number
49. Admitting diagnosis
50. Discharge diagnosis
51–70. Surgery history
       (dates and codes)
71. Smoking, Y or N
72. Comments

MS–2 (I,F,R) Medical staff file (350)

1. Number
2-20. Name, address, memberships, degrees, affiliations, etc.; normal information
21. Date first activity
22. Date last activity
23. Type (courtesy, active, consulting, honorary)
24. Date last appointment
25. Date next appointment
26. Specialty
27. Subspecialty

*I = Input, F = File, R = Report

FIGURE 11–7 Sample File, Input, and Report Requirements

COMMUNITY HOSPITAL
SAMPLE SYSTEM REQUIREMENTS

MEDICAL STAFF AND PATIENT ADMINISTRATION (continued)
MS–2 (I,F,R) Medical staff file (continued)
- 28. Department
- 29. Subdepartment
- 30–35. Original date of 4 standard licenses and 2 certificates
- 36–41. Date last renewal of 4 standard licenses and 2 certificates
- 42–47. Next renewal due of 4 standard certificates
- 48–347. Continuing education and committee meeting hours by category (25) by month for current fiscal year (July–June)
- 348. Year-to-date patient days (automatic update from discharge)
- 349. Year-to-date patient billings (automatic update from discharge)

REPORTS (DBMS)

1. Directories (from any key, selected items in directory)
2. Rolodex cards
3. Mailing—selected keys, personalized letters
4. Mailing labels
5. Exception reports, due date reports
   –license renewals due
   –appointment reviews due
   –Continuing Medical Education status
6. Patient days and billing analysis—various sorts or rankings

MS–3 (I) Admitting (2,100 inpatients, 800 outpatients, and 1,000 emergency room patients per month)

When a patient is admitted, the patient file will be alphabetically searched on-line to see if the patient is on file. File master information (MS–1) will be input for new patients. The preliminary master information will be printed on a form. The patient will verify the information. Changes and additional information necessary for admitting will be input.

FIGURE 11–7 (continued) Sample File, Input, and Report Requirements

RFP Name: _____

RFP EVALUATION   RFP DATE: __ / __ / __   REPLY DATE: __ / __ / __

Vendor: Software _____ , Hardware _____

System Brand _____   Model Number: _____   Date Introduced _____

Hardware Brand Total Mini/Micro Installed _____ Units. This system _____ Units.

Computer Features: Annual DP Revenue $ _____   Yes   Part   No

Word Length: _____ Bits.		Oper. System Firmware		.	.
Operating System: _____ K, _____ User K.		Virtual Memory		.	.
Operating System Name: _____		Variable Length Records		.	.
Partitions: _____ K. Languages: _____		Printer Spooling		.	.
_____		Data Base Management System		.	.
Proposed Software Languages: _____		Word Processing		.	.
_____		Parity or Error Checking		.	.
Source Code? Yes _____ No _____		Simultaneous Jobs/CRT		.	.

Cycle/Access Time ____ / ____ Micro Sec. Maximum Simultaneous Jobs _____ , Programs _____

PROPOSED SYSTEM	BRAND	CAPACITY	MAX UPGRADE	QUAN-TITY	EACH COST	TOTAL COST	MONTHLY COST*
CPU		K	K		$	$	$
Fixed Disk		MB	MB				
Remov. Disk		MB	MB				
Floppy		MB	MB				
Tape		MB	MB				
Communication . .		BAUD	No.				
CRT/VDT		CHAR	No.				
Printers: System:			No.				
Slave:			No.				
Band/Chain . . .		LPM					
Matrix Line		LPM					
Matrix Char . . .		CPS					
Letter Qual		CPS				_____	_____

Total Hardware . . . .

Software . . . . _____

Maintenance . . . .

Monthly Communication . . . . _____

              TOTAL $_____ $_____

*.0 _____ Lease factor

Comments:

FIGURE 11–8 Sample RFP Evaluation Form

RFP Name: Example

RFP EVALUATION   RFP DATE: 1/1/83   REPLY DATE: 2/1/83

Vendor: Software Local Turnkey Vendor , Hardware (Same)

System Brand ABC   Model Number: 20/20   Date Introduced 1978

Hardware Brand Total Mini/Micro Installed 10,000 Units. This system 100 Units.

Computer Features: Annual DP Revenue $ 500,000,000(1)   Yes   Part(6)   No

Word Length: 8 Bits.   Oper. System Firmware(7)   X   .

Operating System: 48(2) K, 0(3) User K.   Virtual Memory   X

Operating System Name: OPOSYS   Variable Length Records   X   .

Partitions: 24(4) K. Languages: _____   Printer Spooling   X   .

   Basic/Cobol   Data Base Management System   X   .   .

Proposed Software Languages: _____   Word Processing.   X   .   .

   Basic   Parity or Error Checking   X   .   .

Source Code? Yes X(5) No _____   Simultaneous Jobs/CRT . (8)   X   .   .

Cycle/Access Time .6/.4 Micro Sec. Maximum Simultaneous Jobs 16 , Programs 16

PROPOSED SYSTEM	BRAND	CAPACITY(9)	MAX UPGRADE(10)	QUAN-TITY(11)	EACH COST(12)	TOTAL COST(13)	MONTHLY COST*(14)
CPU	ABC	96 K	512 K	1	$30,000	$30,000	$ 795
Fixed Disk	"	20 MB	300 MB	1	12,000	12,000	318
Remov. Disk	"	20 MB	300 MB	1	Incl.		
Floppy		1.2 MB	2.4 MB	1	Incl.		
Tape		48 MB	48 MB	1	Incl.		
Communication . .	XYZ	1200 BAUD	16 No.(A)	2	3,000	6,000	159
CRT/VDT	ZYX	1920 CHAR	31 No.(B)	4	1,500	6,000	159
Printers:	System:		1+ No.(C)				
	Slave:		31 No.(D)				
Band/Chain . . .		LPM					
Matrix Line		LPM					
Matrix Char . . .	DEF	120 CPS		2	2,500	5,000	133
Letter Qual	GHI	45 CPS		1	3,000	3,000	79
Total Hardware						62,000	1,643
Software						14,000	371
Maintenance						. . .	500(E)
Monthly Communication						. . .	300
TOTAL						$76,000	$2,814

*.0265   Lease factor

Comments: (See instructions, Figure 11-10)

FIGURE 11-9 Sample Completed RFP Evaluation Form

INSTRUCTIONS FOR SAMPLE RFP EVALUATION FORM

Most items are self-explanatory; clarifications of some items follow:

1. Annual DP revenue of the hardware manufacturer.
2. Total Operating System bytes.
3. Amount used of the CPU main memory capacity listed below.
4. If partition system, amount of main memory per partition.
5. Is source code provided?
6. Partially.
7. Is the operating system in ROM firmware?
8. Can two jobs be performed on one CRT? Sometimes called foreground/background or attach/detach, where an operator can call up a new job on a CRT while the computer is performing or holding the original job, do the second job, and then return to the first, subject to maximum number of simultaneous jobs.
9. Capacity of the proposed system.
10. Maximum upgrade, including compatible lines that require no program changes. Some items: (A) number of communication lines; (B) number of CRTs with one system printer; (C) number of system printers; if CRT and printer ports are interchangeable, enter "1 +" so that No. CRTs plus No. printers equals number of ports; (D) if printers can be driven by means of CRTs, enter number.
11. Quantity proposed referring to capacity.
12. Cost of respective items. If items such as CRTs or printers are included in a bundled price of a CPU, show the incremental cost of a comparable CRT or printer with that item, and subtract that cost to obtain a net effective CPU cost. Include miscellaneous costs with CPU. Exclude installation and tax.
13. (11) × (12)
14. Cost to lease at the lease rate noted. Show maintenance as a total near the bottom. (E)

FIGURE 11–10 Instructions for Figure 11–9

vendor responses. Most professional consulting firms have a form that they use. (The form I developed and use is shown in Fig. 11–8, with a completed sample and instructions following in Figs. 11–9 and 11–10, respectively.) Vendors will provide varying and confusing responses to requirements and requests. Each vendor will tout features that they have. A common format is important to facilitate easy comparison. Larger and more complex projects will require a more comprehensive form for information. As a minimum, you should tabulate and compare the data requested in the Easy Data Computer Comparisons (Tables A2–4 to A2–7) listed in Appendix 2.

Most of the tabulated response data pertains to the hardware. The software capabilities are more important, but more subjective. The response assumes that you meet your software requirements, but verification requires observing actual projects that are similar to the one you have in mind. The important hardware data to tabulate for preliminary evaluation are the unit costs and upgrade capabilities. These will help you identify the expansion capabilities and costs. Some of the most important hardware features relate to simultaneous multiuser activities, print spooling and dual-task capabilities per CRT. Stated speeds or benchmark test comparisons need to be verified by observation.

EVALUATING VENDORS AND BRANDS*

The first step in evaluating potential vendors and brands for a computer system is to evaluate the responses to your request for proposals. Are they professional? Do they address your needs?

You should have met with representatives from the vendors while they were preparing the responses. You should meet with the vendors again to personally discuss their responses. The quality of the people should provide you with your initial clues to selecting a manageable number of vendors for further evaluation. You should be meeting with the people who will be doing the programming and/or training.

Some of the key signs to look for in vendors are:

1. They Listen
   Positive. The vendor listens to your needs and requirements.
   Negative. The vendor's personnel talk about how great they are.
2. They Ask Important Questions
   Positive. They show an interest in your needs and want to learn.
   Negative. They ask rhetorical questions that put you on the defense.
3. They Talk in Your Language
   Positive. You clearly understand their products and service and are able to ask questions for further clarification.
   Negative. Strange words and concepts are used to cover up the

---

*Detailed ratings, test results, prices, and specifications for brands and systems are included in Appendix 2.

salesperson's inability to understand and relate to you. This also makes you uncomfortable and afraid to ask questions.

4. They Are Positive
Positive. They show how jobs will be easier and profits will improve.
Negative. They stress fear and the bad things that will happen if you do not buy their products from them. They make you feel guilty about your present status.

5. They Demonstrate Your Needs
Positive. When they demonstrate their system they have made a sample using real data from your business.
Negative. They try to dazzle you with a canned demonstration with their data.

6. Functional Facilities
Positive. Cost-effective facilities indicate good business judgment, sound financing, and fair pricing.
Negative. Excessively plush facilities indicate high prices or future bankruptcy. Inadequate facilities indicate a lack of both capital and ability to provide service and support.

Investigate the stability and credibility of the potential vendors. An important indication of the stability is the terms of payment. If the sales outlet demands a fast payment to cover its working capital and cash flow requirements, the outlet may not be there the following week.

DEMONSTRATIONS

When you have selected a few vendors for further evaluations, the next step is to observe demonstrations at the vendors' facilities. This is a very important process. You should be prepared to attend several demonstrations of each system you are considering. The steps you should take in preparing for the demonstration process are:

1. Before the actual demonstration and evaluation, it is important to gather and review material on the prospective system. You should review the literature concerning the individual computer system. This allows you to be prepared for the unique or special characteristics of the system and any drawbacks surrounding its use. You should note the basic components, features, and functions of each system. Beware of special features that are not necessary for your

needs. You may be increasing the system cost for a feature that may not be used.

2. You should develop a list of questions to ask during each demonstration. This will save time and allow you to concentrate on the special functions of the systems once your standard checklist has been completed.

3. You should inform the vendor as to the specific software applications you want to review, e.g., word processing, accounting, or electronic spreadsheet.

4. You should bring a standard problem unique to your business. The problem should be small but complex. For word processing the problem may be a form used. For a spreadsheet or graphics application the problem will be a standard table or form. An accounting requirement will include your transactions. Bring this problem to each computer demonstration and use it for product comparison.

5. You should bring writing or taping materials to document thoughts and observations. You may miss certain points or want to comment on the system during the demonstration.

6. You should bring or ask for a price sheet for the system being evaluated. This should have been included in the vendor proposal. During the demonstration you should mark off the items described for an accurate pricing of the system's hardware and software configuration.

7. If the demonstration is moving too quickly, do not hesitate to ask the demonstrator to slow down. A demonstrator is usually comfortable with the demonstration routine and may slide over portions of the demonstration you are interested in evaluating. A slick demonstration may be staged to avoid questions.

8. You should operate the computer and test your problem. Hands-on time is an important part of the demonstration. Do not hesitate to ask the demonstrator if you may step through part of the demonstration yourself or perform some of the functions you are interested in.

ON-SITE EVALUATION

The best evaluation method is to visit some of the vendor's customers. Telephone reference checks can provide some useful insights, but the information will be more limited. Many customers do not know that they paid too much and received too little. They do not know what they could have received. They may be reluctant to admit their mistakes. These factors will be most apparent through comparative on-site visits.

Ask the vendor for the names of customers you can talk to, preferably customers with a system like the one you are considering. When you visit the customer sites, bring a list of questions to ask and items to observe. A sample list is the following:

1. What type of training, instruction, reference, and maintenance logs are given to the customer? What is seen in the showroom may not be given at the site.
2. Ask questions relating to your application and whether the performance is adequate.
3. If they have a similar configuration, observe the application software with multiusers and a full data base to gauge response time. If there were sample data for the software application demonstration in the vendor's showroom, a full data base may considerably slow down the execution of the programs.
4. Review with the customer the software and hardware maintenance and support provided by the vendor. What is the response time? A review of the maintenance log will provide insights concerning hardware reliability.
5. Ask about the quality and the extent of the training policy.

SOFTWARE

After people, software is the most important consideration in a computer system. Software was discussed in detail in Chapter 4.

Purchasing software is one of the most important decisions you will have to make. Business software is less flexible than hardware. For example, if the software you require does exist, it is probably written to run on a specific computer.

When evaluating a vendor's system and software, you should obtain answers to the following questions:

1. What comes standard with the system?
2. How does the software manufacturer handle modifications and updates.
3. If software customization is required, who will do it?

You should carefully review the documentation and manuals for the software packages. Packaged software is usually low in cost and should be proven. If you are considering package software, you should review the number and quality of installations.

Find out the software support policy. Be sure you are adequately covered for updates, current releases, and any software modifications. About 90 percent of maintenance problems are software-related. Make sure thorough software support is provided.

TRAINING

Another important item to evaluate when purchasing a business computer system is the training policy. Without proper and comprehensive training, the potential of your business computer will be underutilized.

Some manufacturers have designed their systems for self-installation and offer no training or marketing support for the very low-priced systems. The training is usually the responsibility of the sales outlet. Be sure to determine the specific charges for training and the number of your people included.

Ask what type or style of training is offered for the customer. Is it performed in a formal classroom environment or on an individual basis? Sometimes video cassettes and/or floppy diskettes and a training manual are used for customer training.

Get clear about what goes into the amount of time spent training each employee and the policy for additional training time. Also, be sure to determine the cost for training additional employees. The additional training time may be significantly higher priced than the initial training period. The customer site evaluation should provide a good indication of the training support.

Check the quality of the training documentation involved in the training session. The documentation will be used as a reference after the training, and directions should be clear and precise. Also, inquire whether the training documentation is included with the price of the system.

A well-designed, thoroughly researched, well-managed, and properly implemented in-house training program can be extremely effective. A business must always contend with the problem of job turnover. By implementing a training program, the employer enables a new employee to learn the system without a large drop in productivity and without additional training costs. A basic list of procedures and a good training manual (with tapes and/or diskettes, if possible) can be effective resources to develop a course. Another source of training and support is the local user groups.

HARDWARE MAINTENANCE

Some key questions that should be answered concerning hardware maintenance are:

1. What is the length of the warranty on a piece of equipment?
2. What does the warranty include?
3. Does the seller offer a maintenance contract?
4. What is the maintenance fee, and what service does it include? A maintenance fee may be a monthly, quarterly, or yearly agreement.
5. What is the service source? Is the service performed by the store, dealer, a third party (TRW, GE), or a manufacturer?
6. Where will the service or maintenance be performed? Is the repair site local?
7. Does the service provider offer loaner units or spare parts kits?
8. What is the standard response time for the maintenance service of the service center on your particular system? The industry standard for larger manufacturers is 4 to 6 hours. Response time turnaround may vary with different computer dealers and retail stores.
9. What additional charges are incurred if service is required beyond that specified in the contract?
10. What are the charges for work performed before or after the standard 8-to-5, Monday-through-Friday, work week?

You should inquire what extra features the service programs offer. Does the service include any board or system swapping? Is there phone inquiry service or a "hot line"? Do you have to self-install the system, or does a technician do this? What levels of diagnostics or testing must you perform before you call your service outlet? Some manufacturers and retail outlets require you to perform simple diagnostics over the phone before a technician will be sent.

Most manufacturers prefer you go to a local service outlet or dealership. The objections to having a machine returned to the factory are simple: time and trouble. It takes time to pack and ship a system back to the manufacturer. Then you must consider the amount of time that you will be without a system. For the most part, manufacturer maintenance should be the last resort.

In addition to the manufacturer and computer stores and dealers, there are third-party maintenance, or independent service, organizations. The most common third-party maintenance companies are TRW, GE, Dow Jones, and Sorbus. These companies usually deal by contract for peripherals and under license to manufacturers. The advantage with these large organizations is convenience (service on site) and availability (nationwide). The disadvantage is usually high overhead that is reflected in your service rate. There are smaller service organizations that are available locally. These smaller organizations may offer an extended warranty rate or one-time charge for time and materials. They may also service more than one manufacturer, either on site or as a carry-in.

You must remember that the least expensive contract may not always guarantee least costs overall. If your business computer system is down a significant amount of time, you will pay through lost labor and mental aggravation.

BRANDS OF COMPUTERS

Current ratings, benchmark test results, prices, specifications, and evaluations for many manufacturers and their systems are included in Appendix 2. This appendix includes instructions on how to evaluate features and compare published specifications. Prices, specifications, and features change rapidly. There is a wide price variation among the systems for comparable apparent or stated features and specifications. Prices for comparably specified systems should be carefully evaluated to assure that value for state-of-the-art features is received.

There are many business computer systems manufacturers, and you should be concerned with a prospective manufacturer's credibility and his specific system's standing in the marketplace. You should inquire what percentage of company sales is involved in the computer industry. Inquire what percentage is in the market segment of the computer industry that the product you are considering is in. You may have doubts about a manufacturer if his involvement is only 20 percent. You should obtain current annual and quarterly reports if the companies are publicly held. If the companies are privately held, they may publish yearly financial statements (unaudited) or provide you with financial information. You should ask how many of the systems and software packages you are considering the manufacturer has installed. The number will indicate the stability and popularity of the system. When was the system first introduced? An older system may not have important new features.

When you buy computer hardware, you are not just buying a computer; you are starting a "system." Your choice should be governed by the system as a whole and how well the system suits your present and anticipated applications. Can the system be expanded to keep pace with your future needs? Can you get the disk drives, modems, additional memory upgrades, etc., that you may need? How easily can you add extra memory, and at what cost? How many companies supply equipment which can be used with this system? Is software available to make the system do what you want and need it to do?

You should observe the physical configuration of the system for functionality and comfort. You should note whether the keyboard is attached or detached. This may be important for operator comfort. You should note the location of the storage media (drives) and whether they are modular. This will be important for upgrading and comfort. You should observe the size and color of the terminal screen. A small screen is difficult to read, and the color of a screen sometimes causes eyestrain.

You should determine whether additional components (peripherals) may be configured with system. Ask whether additional disk drives are available. Does the system have the capability of adding multiple terminals? How many printers may be attached? Is hard-disk storage available for the particular system? Can you expand memory?

You should have specifications of the number of components that may be added to a particular system. These will include the number of disk drives, terminals, and printers that may be configured together. For example, a system may only handle two terminals and one printer or one terminal and two printers. Confirm whether certain interfacing is required to attach additional equipment. This can be a hidden expense.

You should know whether the additional peripherals are supplied by the computer unit manufacturer or another vendor. The peripherals may be supplied from several different manufacturers. Be sure to clarify whether and which additional equipment is compatible with the main unit. Determine whether the manufacturer or the vendor is responsible for the support of these additional components. If the support of the peripherals is good, selection of a variety of them may be advantageous.

The specifications should include whether the system configuration has single-user or multiuser capabilities. A manufacturer may supply both types of systems. Be certain that the system you purchase can be upgraded to a multiuser system if that is the type of system you may need in the future.

IBM

It is impossible to discuss hardware brands without special emphasis on IBM. IBM's 1982 data processing sales were $30 billion, 7.5 times that of the next largest competitor, DEC. IBM's volume is more than the total of the next fifteen largest computer companies and represents approximately 36 percent of the total U.S. computer hardware industry.

Computer industry customers and vendors, along with security analysts and lenders, carefully watch IBM's product and marketing moves. Because of its size, it seems capable of doing many things no other company can do. Surprisingly, however, IBM has been having a declining impact on the computer industry.

I personally believe that IBM is one of the best managed large companies. I believe that the anti-trust cases against IBM were unwarranted, as evidenced by the large number of competitors in all segments of the computer industry. IBM's corporate policies have been to promote competition and free enterprise within the industry. (This is contrary to the policies of the leading companies in many other major industries. Many industries have trade associations and government lobbying groups to promote "standardization." In addition, the companies have a follow-each-other attitude [don't rock the boat] in policies concerning products, pricing, marketing, and labor relations.)

During the past few years there have been numerous discussions and articles in the computer profession about IBM's marketing and retaliation tactics. IBM, of course, uses the power of its size and available advertising dollars. IBM salespeople use psychology and pressure to their advantage.

A common technique is to direct personal attention and advertising to the people at a higher level than the computer user. IBM salespeople will use the psychological technique of fear of not being with the best, e.g., "We are the biggest, therefore we must be the best. (!?)" The publicized retaliation techniques include IBM salespeople going to the boss of the DP professional who selected another brand and raising questions concerning the DP professional's competence. Another technique is to raise the same questions to potential employers to create a job market blacklist.

Some IBM salespeople will direct this psychological fear to the DP professionals themselves: "What if you fail by not going with us? What will your boss think? How many jobs will be available to you if you fail? If you have IBM experience, there are a lot more jobs for you!"

I do not believe that there is any IBM policy to encourage the previously mentioned high-pressure sales practices. These practices are the result of a large sales force of diversified individuals. Some individuals will use any tactic at their disposal to obtain short-term results.

Some of the same sales pressure techniques may be applied to consultants and teachers. In addition, many of these "professionals" in the computer field cannot, or by choice do not, keep up with the rapid change in available products. The "safe" recommendation, therefore, is always to use the products of the biggest company.

In addition, many of the large professional firms and educational institutions are "establishment oriented." They believe that good products come from what they call "proper planning" according to the procedures in the books they read and write. They do not believe (or maybe, do not want to believe) that the free-wheeling, entrepreneurial, seat-of-the-pants planning style of many of the new companies can develop and support technologically advanced, quality products.

Many of the best small-business computer products come from newer companies, not from IBM. Nearly every purchaser of computer products compares the product he or she purchases against IBM products. The newer small companies are also up against the formidable, previously mentioned selling techniques and pressures. These companies, therefore, could not exist if they did not have better products. Many companies have entered the business and failed; however, the total number of companies has continually increased since the inception of the industry. IBM's sales have not grown as rapidly as the total computer industry, and especially the small-business-computer segment of the industry.

Small-business computers account for less than 15 percent of IBM's sales. IBM's major product line is the multimillion-dollar large-mainframe computers. These computers represent the largest segment of the computer industry, although this segment is not growing as rapidly as that represented by the small-business computers. Because of the total size of this market segment and the stiff competition, however, large-mainframe computers must receive the focus of attention of IBM's top management.

IBM's impact on the small computers in terms of product innovation and quality is that of follower, not leader. IBM has had a powerful influence in marketing due to the strength of its name and the financial and personnel resources it possesses. The corporation waits until a given market segment is large enough to warrant its attention, and then it enters the market with a strong marketing program.

IBM entered the rapidly growing personal computer field in 1981 with a strong marketing and advertising program. (The 5100 series of computers introduced in 1975 were personal computers in terms of features and capability, but were higher priced.) Because of its name, IBM, of course, received a great deal of free publicity from the press. I believe that the primary effect of IBM's entry into this market will be to add credibility and respectability to this market segment. The leaders in the personal computer market, Apple and Radio Shack, will not suffer. IBM's impact will be to expand the market.

IBM's follower strategy has certainly been successful in terms of obtaining market share, but the effects of their products' below average technology and quality, along with sales personnel tactics, have left a somewhat tarnished image in the small- to medium-sized business community. Consider, for example, the following quotes, excerpted from a May 3, 1982 article in *Computerworld*. The article is by Hillel Segal, president of the Association of Computer Users. This association conducts performance tests (called "benchmark tests") on the many brands of computers, and the article summarized the results of tests on small IBM computers.

> A slow performance in the accounting problem and mediocre scientific/engineering test performance. . . . But overall quality of keyboard and screen was considered excellent, as was the system documentation.
>
> A bug discovered in the unit's processing of certain arithmetic operations clouds the horizon, . . .
>
> David S. Wolaneck discovered the bug when his program called for division of .1 by 10. The computer's answer was .001, erring in placement of the decimal point. We understand that IBM acknowledged existence of the bug.
>
> In this issue we are covering results of the IBM 5120 as well as the Personal Computer. The 5120 is no longer offered by IBM; the system was so short-lived that by the time the ACU had published its benchmark report the system had been outmoded by the introduction of the IBM Datamaster and the Personal Computer. . . .
>
> The IBM 5120 replaced IBM's earlier small system entry, the 5110, . . .
>
> . . . a check of several local customers indicated general satisfaction. . . .
>
> Of course, IBM will have to do something about the recently reported arithmetic bug. As Mr. Wolaneck commented, "Everyone assumes that computers do arithmetic correctly." No question about that, I'm sure, even at IBM.

The following excerpts are from an article by Mr. Segal that appeared in the June 15, 1981 issue of *Computerworld*. The article covered the benchmark tests on the IBM Series/1 for computers in the $25,000 to $50,000 range.

> . . . Unfortunately, our consultants ran into a number of problems in executing their speed tests on the Series/1.
>
> . . . This setup resulted in an unexplained loss of characters in the order entry application.
>
> . . . our consultants concluded that EDL is the "language of choice" . . . IBM's Cobol, on the other hand, was rated by users either "fair" or "poor."

. . . Software support was rated as being somewhat spotty.

. . . Documentation for the Series/1 consists of several hundred pages and is nearly as complex as the system itself.

. . . The problems our consultants encountered reinforces the belief that experienced IBM programmers are a necessity for enjoying the Series/1 to its maximum.

. . . that prevented our consultants from completing the benchmark tests, this may or may not be indicative of IBM's commitment to support users.

We've given IBM a standing offer to rerun the tests if they would provide us with technical support.

IBM introduced the System/38 in 1978 to offer a more technologically competitive computer than its System/34 (first delivery, 1977) in the $50,000 to $300,000 business-computer system market. The first System/38 was delivered more than one year behind schedule in August 1980. Much of the software was also more than a year behind schedule, and many users complained of extensive conversion problems.

IBM will continue to be a major factor in the small-business computer market. Any user or competitor in this market should be aware of IBM's products and its marketing strategy. IBM will have good products and support for many customers. A computer product should be compared against an IBM product, but IBM may not be the best standard of comparison for any specific product.

RATINGS AND EVALUATIONS

Ratings and evaluations of manufacturers and their systems are included in Appendix 2, titled "Hardware Brands and Systems."

13

IMPLEMENTING A COMPUTER SYSTEM

THE CONTRACT

You have decided to buy a computer. The smooth-talking salesman, who has become your "trust-me friend," has a contract for you to sign. Should you sign it? NO!

In fact, one of the first things you should do when you are considering prospective computer vendors is to ask for their standard contracts and terms and conditions (T&Cs). You should also ask if these terms and conditions are negotiable. If they are not, find another vendor. Most reputable vendors do have negotiable terms and conditions.

Read the terms and conditions, ask questions concerning the most obvious items, and ask how your primary concerns will be handled.

The standard T&Cs on most computer-vendor-prepared contracts are pages of fine print designed specifically to protect themselves from being sued by you. If their products will do all the wonderful things they promised, why do they need this contract?

Towards the end of the fine print in most lengthy T&Cs is a statement:

> *The foregoing warranties are in lieu of all other warranties of seller with respect to the equipment, express or implied, and any implied warranties of merchantability and of fitness for a particular purpose shall be inapplicable.*

This (or minor variations) seems to be the favorite phrase of vendors' contract attorneys. It is hard to believe that many buyers actually sign these agreements.

If you have not deciphered the above phrase (they deliberately make such phrases difficult to understand), what it means is:

> *Only the promises* [none] *in these terms and conditions mean anything; any statements or promises made by a representative of the computer company are void; the equipment is not guaranteed to process your data or give you useful reports, or even be suitable for that purpose.* [The equipment will hum when you plug it in.]

And, of course, the contract goes on to say that you must pay in full as soon as *they* plug the machine in and *they* "certify" it works (hums) properly. They may even test it with *their* (not your) data and show that the printer prints *their* data.

Obviously these T&Cs were prepared by the vendors' attorneys for the specific purpose of protecting the vendors. Reputable vendors, however, do not need this protection and will sign an agreement saying they will deliver what they promised.

In previous chapters we stressed the importance of buying turnkey systems or software in conjunction with hardware. ("Turnkey" means you "turn the key" and the computer processes your data—the system must have been tested with your data, and some of your data must have been loaded into the computer prior to delivery.) Obviously, the vendor's standard contract is not applicable to this situation.

We stated earlier that you should not consider a vendor whose contract and T&Cs are not negotiable. Therefore, we assume that the terms are negotiable and that you are now ready to make a deposit and issue a purchase order. *You* are paying; therefore, *you* should control the terms and conditions.

It may be worthwhile for you to prepare the agreement. Keep it simple, and make sure all promises made by the vendor are included.

It may be expedient to use the vendor's standard form, strike all items you do not like (make sure all clauses such as the one we mentioned earlier are removed) and state, "The attached addendum takes precedence over any item in the vendor-prepared documents." You should then prepare an addendum covering all items that you feel are necessary to protect yourself.

Some of the key items you should consider including in the written agreement are:

1. **RFP Requirements.** The software (processing performance) requirements and volumes you prepared prior to receiving quotes.
2. **Vendor Response.** The vendor's written response to those requirements.
3. **Specifications.** The vendor-prepared software specifications and documents.
4. **Item Prices.** Detailed lists of the hardware and software items and prices.
5. **Item Price Adjustments.** Your right to delete or add items at existing prices, prior to delivery and acceptance of the entire system.
6. **Payment Schedule.** Keyed to performance by the vendor. Even with a good turnkey system, it takes time for training and installation of all systems. You should not pay for software modules prior to complete testing and acceptance. If the system is large, you will probably not need all the terminals and printers until all applications are running smoothly. *Do not agree to finance a vendor's working capital!*
7. **Acceptance Criteria.** Should be clearly defined.
8. **Software Rights.** Your right to modify and use the software you buy, including the "source" code that enables another programmer to interpret and modify the programs.
9. **Source Code Escrow.** If the source code is not provided, a copy should be placed in escrow for you to receive if the vendor discontinues business or fails to give you adequate support.
10. **Copyright Infringement Protection.** You should have protection if the software the vendor provides is found to infringe other people's copyrights.
11. **Cancellation.** If the agreement is cancelled for any reason, you are liable only for expenses incurred.
12. **Equipment Capacity.** The equipment will process the volumes presented and will have excess capacity for a stated percentage growth.
13. **Operating Response Time.** The system will give certain results within a given amount of time after operator entry. This is especially important in a multiuser system.
14. **Performance Milestones.** If check dates for the vendor to complete certain activities are not met, the agreement is cancelled and the vendor must refund all monies. There may be a provision for certain charges to be paid on a time and material basis.

15. **Documentation and Training.** The vendor will provide necessary documentation and training.
16. **Maintenance Rates.** Should cover the monthly charge and the period for which it is guaranteed. Must include both hardware and software.
17. **Maintenance Response Time.** Maximum number of hours after you call for maintenance before a maintenance person will be at your site to fix your equipment and/or software.
18. **Downtime.** The maximum number of continuous hours your system will be inoperable.
19. **Backup and/or Replacement.** If any of the previous conditions are not met, the vendor should provide a backup system and, with repeated failures, replace the system or refund your money.

These items are certainly not exhaustive, and additional considerations will be determined by the specific nature and magnitude of the project. Competent legal advice may be one of your best investments. Computer law and potential problems have many unique characteristics; we recommend you consult with an expert in the field, a specialty for which many attorneys do not have the proper expertise.

Contract terms and conditions are a necessary evil, and you hope you will never need to refer to them. Common sense and careful reference checks are your best protection.

Unfortunately, there are many problems and lawsuits in the industry. Many experts are predicting a large number of lawsuits in the 1980s. This will be a result of heavy competition in the rapidly growing small-business computer market. Vendors will be making promises they cannot fulfill, and products will be sold that have not been fully tested.

If you have signed a vendor-prepared contract, it does not mean you have lost all rights. Many times these contracts serve only to intimidate the buyer and do not stand up in court. Many buyers, when they read the fine print after they have a problem, think that they have signed away their rights. Many courts, however, have upheld the "express and implied warranties" that the salesman made and have awarded damages to the buyer. You should keep documentation of all promises.

As with any agreement, it is best to have all understandings spelled out clearly in a written document. Proceed with caution. Working with a vendor who provides an agreement that favors you—requires payments only on the basis of value received and tested and, in essence, "satisfaction guaranteed"—is your key to success.

HUMAN FACTORS IN IMPLEMENTATION

Some businesses that have recently purchased a business computer have experienced office workers with frazzled nerves crying at the end of the day. Office worker turnover can increase to 75 percent the first year, and the company's records can be in worse shape than they were B.C. (Before Computer). Employee productivity and morale may be much lower.

Many businesses have installed business computer systems with minimal problems. Their employees willingly work overtime and look forward to creating documents and special reports using word processing and data base management. Usually, no employees have been laid off; however, in some cases sales volume has doubled in two years with no increase in office personnel, and turnover has been minimal. The tedious, monotonous jobs are now performed by the computer, and management has detailed and summary information that has helped improve customer service while reducing receivable and inventory ratios and increasing gross profit margins.

You may have noticed that we said the businesses with problems "purchased a computer" and the successful businesses "installed a computer system." Successfully installing an office automation system requires careful planning, realistic expectations, and the involvement of all key personnel.

Almost every office is already in the process of becoming the "office of the future." Most offices have a copying machine, electronic calculators, and self-correcting typewriters. Many now have computerized telephone systems. Many utilize outside computer, printing, and microfilming services.

Offices are rapidly adding small-business, word processing, engineering, and graphics computers. Cost-effective electronic typewriters have been introduced. Computer data storage costs and processing capabilities continue to improve dramatically while declining in price. There will be increased use of computer and audio-visual communication networking, including electronic (and laser) photocopying, reduction (including miniaturization), and enlargement.

The office of the future involves computerized filing, calculating, typing (word processing), communicating, duplicating, and information retrieval. Less storage space will be required, and jobs will be done more quickly.

INCREASED PRODUCTIVITY

The office of the future will still have people, but the people will have tools to be more productive and to improve communication. The office of the future means increased office worker productivity and increased managerial efficiency. It also means improved utilization of scarce resources—the scarcest being educated, talented human beings. Since it is becoming increasingly difficult to find qualified, educated people, we must better utilize the ones we have.

There is a need for more work by educated individuals than can possibly be accomplished, even with dramatic increases in productivity, for at least the next century and probably forever. There will always be work to do for those who want to work. There is no reason to fear increased productivity. It can only mean a higher standard of living or, for those who choose, more leisure time.

EVOLUTION OF AUTOMATION

Office automation has evolved gradually, without radical changes in the way things are done. This will continue. The "office of the future" is not a static, well-defined structure. It is, in fact, an office that is changing. It will be more of an environment than a physical structure. It will be an environment that facilitates and promotes change, growth, and increased productivity.

Implementing increased productivity tools into the office may be done gradually, with minimal disruptions. Some tools, such as a new copier or telephone system, may be easy to learn and use.

There will be certain systems that increase productivity that will require major capital investments and major changes in the way things are done. This is usually the case with a full business computer system. Because of the computer memory capability (it does not forget instructions) and ability to do mundane tasks extremely fast, things can, and should, be done much differently than they were done manually.

The implementation of a computer system will take place somewhat gradually. It takes time to plan and test and to train people to operate and use a computer system. Some activities will be performed in parallel prior to full conversion.

MYTH OF WORKER RESISTANCE

One of the first steps in a successful office automation project is to realize that worker fears and resistance are a myth. The workers will welcome the project! They will help you if they are involved, because most people welcome using new tools.

Given the choice of going from California to New York by walking or by piloting a modern jet, most people will prefer piloting the jet. They, of course, must learn to fly the jet; they would prefer to walk rather than be sent up in the air alone and untrained. They would, however, look forward to the exciting new experience of learning to fly this powerful machine.

Most people doing detailed, monotonous jobs do not want to be doing the same thing every day for the rest of their life. People want and enjoy change. They enjoy utilizing new tools.

The only ones who want to do the same thing every day for the rest of their lives are the ones who have reached their "Peter Principle" level of incompetence. This is generally at the management, not bottom worker, level.

Some managers are afraid of new technologies they do not understand. Sometimes managers will not see the new tools their workers will be using. Some managers have self-doubts about their abilities to manage in a different environment. Sometimes they are afraid of a subordinate who knows more about a new technology than they know. Some managers know how they used to do the job, but fear that they will not know how to manage their subordinates in the future.

MANAGEMENT EDUCATION

The first key step in implementing a major increased office productivity system such as a business computer is management involvement, education, and attitude adjustment. Top management must be dedicated to increasing productivity and using the most cost-effective tools available.

Top management does not need to understand the electronic and optical intricacies of how these tools work. They should, however, understand how these tools are operated and what their capabilities are.

If you have a new remote-controlled color television with digital channel selector, you do not need to know the inner workings. You just need to know what it can do and which buttons to push.

The best way to learn about office automation products is to visit a few showrooms and push the buttons. Trade shows offer an opportunity to see many products and push buttons in one location. Personal computers have limited use in many offices, but offer an excellent method of learning computer operation and capabilities at home.

PLANNING AND INVOLVEMENT

At the beginning we discussed "implementing a system" rather than "purchasing" a piece of equipment. "Purchasing" implies ordering and accepting delivery without modifications or training. "Implementing" a system requires designing, planning, some custom tailoring, and installation training and scheduling.

It is important to have a plan. As you automate your office, you will be integrating many systems and procedures. You must know how all the pieces will fit together. You must know how to position yourself for greater changes.

All employees who will be managing, operating, or using information from a new system should be involved in the planning and implementation. This should start at the top. All these people should be involved in developing the plan.

The plan may be brief, but it should be in writing. Some of the best input may come from the potential operators. The tools will need operators, and the operators must work together and know what they are trying to accomplish. The current workers and potential operators will welcome the opportunity to provide input and will feel a stronger sense of involvement when the training and installation begin.

It is best to have the final plan reviewed and approved by the top manager and the key managers and advisors who have responsibility for what the system produces and who have an overview of the total system. A small group at this point is important for justifying the plan and establishing responsibilities and priorities.

When an office automation system vendor is selected, the vendor's personnel planning, support, training, and implementation capability must be a consideration. A key coordinator, whether on your staff, the vendor's staff, or an independent consultant is important in assuring total involvement, training, and coordination.

The "office of the future" implies continued change and utilization of productivity tools. Progress is change; increased productivity is change. The only thing to fear is attempted stagnation. In a dynamic total environment, you can only move forward or decay. The "office of the future," through the use of tools, means more productive, meaningful, and enjoyable jobs.

INSTALLATION AND TRAINING

Installation of a computer system and training personnel to operate and use a computer system almost always take longer and are more difficult than the purchaser expects. Converting activities from a manual process to computer or converting computer systems is a complex project. Problems can be minimized with careful planning and anticipation of potential problems. The first step is to be aware of the scope and complexity of the project.

The basic purpose of implementing any increased productivity system is to change and improve the way things are done. You do not want just to do things faster: when things can be done faster, they should be done differently and better.

Implementing a computer system or changing a computer system should involve major changes in many activities and procedures. Sometimes changing computer systems will be a more complex project than installing the initial computer. When systems are being changed, it should be because the new system offers significant advantages and capabilities over the previous system.

Installing the initial small-business computer, which costs less than $20,000, is equivalent to hiring and training between ten and one hundred people. Installing a larger system or converting a system is even more complex.

After identifying the scope and complexity of the project, the next step is to develop a plan. This plan should identify what event has to be done by whom, when it has to be completed, and which events have to be completed before other events can start. The plan can be a listing of events with a starting date, completion date, and person responsible. A bar chart may be useful for visually presenting the events in the project.

Experienced vendors often have a planning format and procedure. You should review a vendor's planning documents and procedures when you evaluate the vendor.

A key item that can be very time-consuming in implementing or converting a system is the preparation of the software and processing specifications and documents, which include training manuals. A good vendor will have these prepared prior to implementation. The vendor should have these items for custom or modified software in a word processing file so they can be easily and quickly updated. Processing run sheets or checklists can be very useful for controlling the computer operations. These specifications and documents will facilitate implementation and training, and they are extremely important for future training of new personnel. Their absence exposes a computerized organization to considerable problems when unforeseen personnel turnover occurs.

It will take time to load all the necessary data into the computer files. Codes need to be assigned to all records. The coding system should be carefully developed to facilitate easy use and future expansion. The computer system will create considerable extra work during this period. If this extra work is anticipated and properly performed, it will substantially reduce future personnel work.

Testing is extremely important and takes time. A new system

should be tested with a small amount of test data prior to complete conversion. Initial testing should be performed at the vendor's facility prior to delivery of the equipment. Testing procedures and acceptance criteria should be included in both the implementation plan and the contract.

Parallel processing is not usually required for most applications. In fact, it should not be required. Parallel processing was a common procedure in the early days of computer systems because then a computer system duplicated, but efficiently automated, the previous system. Computer system reliability was suspect, and parallel runs provided a good testing procedure. Current computer systems are much more powerful and reliable than the early computer systems. Applications (e.g., payroll) should be performed differently to maximize the usefulness of a new computer system. When the application is performed differently, parallel processing comparisons to the old procedures and reports may not be possible. It is very easy, and also important, to include control reports and totals within an application system. These controls make parallel processing unnecessary and will assure accuracy and control in the future. If parallel processing is required, it means that you will not be sure of future accuracy, after parallel processing is discontinued.

Implementing a new computer system or converting a computer system is a major project. Any major project, when carefully planned and controlled, can be very rewarding for the people involved. When results are planned on an event/milestone basis and the results are achieved, each milestone accomplishment will be personally rewarding.

SECURITY CONSIDERATIONS

Computer crimes are increasing and receiving much publicity. The increase is a result of the fact that the amount of data computerized is more than doubling every year. Although computer crimes are up, the rate of increase is substantially less than the rate of growth in computer use. The news that has not been widely reported, and for which the details are not available, is that so-called "computer crimes" have been more than offset by computer controls substantially reducing many losses and "white collar crimes!"

The computer crimes that receive the greatest notoriety are the ones relating to the financial industry involving the electronic transfer of funds. The best publicized ones (such as the recent Security Pacific and Wells Fargo cases) involved millions of dollars, but the perpetrators were caught, and most of the funds were recovered. Some of the smaller cases that have been publicized are: the teller who transferred funds from dormant accounts to his account; the person who left his computer-coded deposit slips on the counter for others to fill out; and the programmer who had the computer round up individuals' payroll deductions, accumulating a large excess over the total, and credited his account for the difference.

Newspapers, magazines, and television leave the impression many times that these are only the cases that were caught or disclosed, and that there may be many others that were not caught or were caught and not disclosed. It makes interesting reading, and it helps perpetuate a certain fear of computers.

The facts are that most computerized businesses, and especially financial institutions, have accurate and timely computer reports showing shortages and out-of-balance ledgers and accounts, along with key ratios and indexes indicating abnormalities. Before computers existed, some of the largest losses in financial institutions were caused by human errors in making change and posting accounts. This does not include the interest lost due to delays in transferring and posting funds.

When customers receive change and there are errors in their favor, and they accept the error, is that a crime? Similarily, when pricing or addition errors are made on customers' invoices or account statements in their favor and they accept the errors, is that a crime? If these are called "white collar crimes," then, in total, white collar crimes have been substantially reduced by computers.

Fortunately, most businesses are not susceptible to the well-publicized kinds of computer crimes. Most businesses do not have the financial exposure caused by the computer transferring of funds. All businesses, however, can profit from the use of timely and accurate computer information to substantially reduce transaction errors.

The computer security concerns of most businesses relate to the loss and misuse of information. Data in a computer can be very quickly erased, either deliberately or inadvertently by people, or because of a machine malfunction. When many employees are using a computer, an unauthorized employee may be able to access some classified information.

These problems also exist with a noncomputerized system, except they take somewhat different forms. It takes longer and is more difficult to burn files, but it is easy to misplace or lose a file or key report. It is easy for anyone to see or pick up information that is laying around or in an unlocked file cabinet.

Accessing unauthorized computer data is much more difficult than accessing normal written or typed information for the average person. It is very easy to design codes or "passwords" into a computer system so that only designated people can access certain information. With this procedure, a person may use the computer system, but be able to access only a limited amount of data within the system and have limited capability in what he or she can do to the data.

Although data can easily be destroyed, it is easier to copy large volumes of data. Therefore, you can have multiple copies (called "backup") of all files. These can be on small plastic disks or tape cassettes. One small tape cassette can hold the equivalent of one four-drawer file cabinet. Backup copies can be kept in fireproof safes or off-site.

The most frequent computer security problems incurred by most small businesses with a computer relate to people, not the computer. The greatest problem is depending on one person or an outside vendor. If a company lets it happen, one employee can control all the records, and this person's disappearance would create a long period before the business could function as it did when the person was there. (However, the business would probably be better off in the long run.)

The same situation can occur without a computer. This is the situation where the controller, office manager, or head bookkeeper has an office piled with papers, does not delegate activities, and is the only one who knows where everything is located and how the pieces fit together.

In any case, the most efficient and least vulnerable organizations are the ones where day-to-day activities run smoothly, even when key people take vacations. Activities must be delegated, and employees are cross-trained. Key procedures must be documented and not be in just one person's head.

The primary security features in a computer system are in the software, not in the hardware. The security features should be an important consideration when evaluating software packages or designing custom software systems.

The password system is the most important feature. Most good software has a multilevel password system. A more cumbersome system than the multilevel system is for each activity to be assigned a list of specific passwords that allow the performance of that activity.

In a multilevel password system, one person will have the highest level (e.g., "10") and have access to everything and be able to do anything. Every activity and file will have a lower level (e.g., "1" to "9") assigned to it. Only the assigned level or higher may perform that activity. A terminal code may also be assigned to lock out certain activities from certain terminals.

Another important feature may be the audit trail maintained by the system. An audit trail system maintains a log of who (by password) did what, when, and on which terminal. This log is usually printed daily.

After a system is implemented, the key security items to evaluate are:

1. **Password Access.** Who controls and reviews the assigned passwords and maintains these passwords in the system? How often?
2. **Daily Log.** Is the log reviewed and monitored by two people? The top person in the organization should be receiving a copy for periodic random reviews and for questioning. A key subordinate should be reviewing and monitoring the log in detail on a daily basis.
3. **System Security.** Is access to the computer or computer room controlled? Does the system have a key lock? Who keeps the keys and where? Where are the disks and/or tapes stored?
4. **Personnel Procedures.** Are people cross-trained? What would happen if a key person had an accident and died? Do key people take vacations, and do things run smoothly when they are gone?
5. **System and Procedures Documentation.** Are all systems and procedures documented? Are the documents clear and concise?
6. **Backup Procedures.** How often is what data backed up? Are duplicate copies maintained off-site? Who has access to these records?

7. **What-if Analysis.** This is often the best security review. What would happen if we had a fire? If someone wanted to cause a problem? If a key person quit? If someone accidentally did something? If someone obtained this information? And so on.

Security with a computer system is a major concern for business, but it should not be a major worry. Most of the worry comes from the mystique of the new technology and the nonvisibility of the electronic information. With proper procedures, security will actually improve with a computer system. These procedures should be frequently, thoroughly, and professionally reviewed and evaluated. Computers are just another facet of the business organization. As with any other facet, "insurance" investments (precaution, planning, action versus reaction management, and all the other buzzwords) can be your best and most important investments.

14

USING COMPUTER PROFESSIONALS

THE DATA PROCESSING DEPARTMENT SYNDROME

The following article by William E. Blundell appeared on the editorial page of the July 7, 1981 edition of *The Wall Street Journal.**

THE SOFTWARE KID INVEIGHS AGAINST THE WITCH DOCTORS

MANAGER'S JOURNAL by William E. Blundell

SAN FRANCISCO—The software kid slips in from the street, wraps himself around a Scotch and utters heresy against his clients.

The kid, a private consultant, advises top U.S. corporations about using computers and data processing. He also keeps close ties with the entrepreneurial Wunderkinder of the Silicon Valley, font of many of the newest ideas and gadgets.

And big companies he's seen don't know how to use either, the kid complains. "The greatest thing that could happen," he says, "would be to cut their data processing budgets 75 percent. Then they'd have to discover that there are ways they could do the same job, maybe a better job, on what's left."

The kid is not a hardware salesman, though advising clients on equipment is a key part of his work. Software, which he does sell, is the set of instructions that tells the computer how to do a specific job—keeping inventory, say, or billing you for something you never bought and dunning you remorselessly despite your protests. (I once tangled with an oil company computer that insisted for months I was actually a deadbeat named Blumberg, but that's another story.)

At most firms, computer functions are concentrated in one spot under one control—"the witch doctors of the data systems department," the kid calls them. This department, he adds, is the biggest roadblock to data processing efficiency; most of his client contacts are frustrated managers in financial and other staff departments who can't get what they need from the witch doctors, and enlist his help.

This makes him unpopular. The data systems people in one client company recently derided him as a charlatan and said the small, inexpensive computers he was recommending were toys that wouldn't work. "It's all politics," mutters the kid. "These guys are protecting their turf. They want everyone coming to them, completely dependent on them; that's their power base." Meanwhile, he charges, they are wasting millions by loading up on unneeded central computer capacity and hiring armies of in-house technicians to serve it.

These bloated technical empires first began to sprout when computers were huge and very expensive; physically, it made sense to keep them in one place, in special controlled environments, and economically it was desirable to have a central staff control their use to keep them busy around the clock. But as computers got smaller, cheaper and much easier to use, the data systems departments only got bigger, more bureaucratic and more firmly in control.

Managers in other departments now realize something is wrong, but they're often hamstrung in trying to do anything about it, says the kid. "Corporate staff ceded an enormous amount of responsibility to data systems; now they can't get it back. The customer may know what he wants but he can't answer the experts when they say, 'It can't be done.' The data systems people can put the kibosh on anything they want."

Because they have all the specialized knowledge, the data managers are often left largely unmanaged themselves, and waste and error can flourish unheeded. In one company, the kid found an IBM 360 mainframe computer operating on programs devised for an ancient punch card machine, which is like killing a fly by firing a 155–mm. howitzer at it. In another, some 400 programmers are on the payroll; the kid can't figure out what 350 of them do for a living.

Corporate misuse of programmers is common, he notes. A programmer himself, he maintains the job is more art than science. Typically, however, big teams are put to work on a project by assigning each member a tiny piece of the jigsaw. Often their efforts don't mesh, any more than would the work of 20 painters who were each asked to do a little piece of the Mona Lisa.

Drawing down another Scotch, the kid also accuses data systems chiefs of ignoring the savings and efficiency that small computers could bring—in part because the new machines, operable with little employee training and dispersed among user departments to do specific jobs, would erode data systems' corporate clout.

"Instead," he says disgustedly, "they just buy the next generation IBM mainframe. You wind up with a bunch of Cunard liners that can cross an ocean but can't get into your harbor. You need rowboats for that." A common objection by data systems to small computers is that they are limited in function and wouldn't be kept busy enough, an argument that sends the kid up the wall. "If something costs only $3,500 and you save $100,000 a year with it, what the hell does it matter that you use it only five minutes a day?" he asks.

New ideas sometimes have to be disguised and smuggled past the in-house experts. Working for a big utility's accounting department, the kid was opposed by data systems when he recommended that the accountants use their own small computers to handle accounts payable. Conversion would take a year, the experts intoned, and the equipment might not work. The kid says the accountants got their computers by calling them "electronic calculators"; they were put on line in 60 days, and the cost of doing the work has dropped to a fraction what it was.

Foreign firms seem to appreciate the small computers' potential more than most U.S. firms do, he says. One company in Silicon Valley he has ties to is shipping about half its output abroad, largely to Germany. "They're lean and keen over there. We're fat and constipated," he laments.

None of this makes a lot of difference to the kid financially. A hired gun, he gets paid whether client companies take his advice or not, though he makes more if he gets to install systems he suggests. What really bothers the kid, who is on the shady side of 40 now and getting long in the tooth for the computer racket, is all the botched opportunities and waste. "The thing people wanted from computers they're just not getting," he sighs. "And they could have it. They could have it."

The corporate data processing department industry is plagued with high personnel turnover. The computer experts who work for the large companies and jump from company to company seem more concerned with the appearance of their resumes than with anything else. They believe that the good-looking resume and personal salary market value depend on state-of-the-art experience and responsibility over or with a large system, a large budget, and a large staff. These experts have a powerful influence over a business's stages of computer systems growth. Common stages of growth are:

1. A business buys a computer system from a manufacturer. The system includes accounting software packages such as general ledger, payroll, accounts payable, and accounts receivable. It takes more than one year to get these packages to operate at a mediocre level of usefulness. High cost-effective potential projects are not implemented.

2. The business hires a programmer with the title of "Data Processing Manager." This programmer starts a few disjointed software projects with no formal plan or design.

3. The projects are behind schedule, so the DP Manager hires a programmer. (Now the first programmer really is a manager on his resume.) More disjointed software projects are now in process.

4. The DP Manager is receiving signs of employer dissatisfaction with his work; however, his resume looks good, so he takes another job. A new DP Manager with an impressive resume is hired.

5. The new DP Manager immediately finds that the software projects are not being done properly and the computer hardware is too small and is not right for the desired applications. A new computer (hardware) is acquired. New, "important" projects are identified and started, and additional programmers are hired by the manager.

6. Projects continue behind schedule. Go back to step 4. (This is called a "loop" in a computer program.)

USING CONTRACT SOFTWARE
PROFESSIONALS

The best way to avoid this "data processing department syn-drome" is to not have a data processing department. Systems should be properly implemented on a turnkey basis. Software projects should be acquired on a contract basis from professionals with the appropriate specialty experience.

In Chapter 4 we discussed the procedures for selecting and managing contract programmers.

MANAGING THE DATA
PROCESSING DEPARTMENT

When a business's data processing operation and budget are large, the business may find it cost effective to have a professional data processing manager and department. The manager should be carefully selected. The manager's background should emphasize accomplishment and contributions to increases in total business profitability.

There are many excellent and conscientious managers in the computer industry. Unfortunately, they seem to be the exception rather than the rule. The sign of a good manager is one who gets projects done on time and within budget. He should be using outside specialists on a selective, cost-effective basis. The data processing budget as a percentage of sales should be de-clining. The manager should have a general understanding of the total company business and be involved in all management aspects of the business. Detailed computer experience may be helpful for this manager, but it is not as important as these other factors.

The top management of a business must be involved in the data processing department management. Top management does not need to understand the details of how the computer works. They do need to understand the objectives and purposes of proj-ects in process. Performance needs to be reviewed, monitored, and carefully evaluated. Good DP management should be rec-ognized and rewarded.

USING A CONSULTANT

Independent computer consulting is a relatively new, and unregulated, profession. This lack of regulation naturally increases competition and quality at the top. Unfortunately, there are many unqualified people calling themselves professional computer consultants. Many are actually salesmen or programmers using a ruse to get in the door. There is also no such thing as "independent" consulting coming from a sales organization or broker, because discounts, commissions, and finders' fees are very volume-oriented, and knowledge will be limited to the brands represented.

Many computer firms offer "free" consulting services. The consultants in these firms usually find that the company that employs them has just what you need. Some cynics think that, as a rule, these "consultants" recommend the largest (most expensive) system they think you will buy.

Many "independent" consultants try to sell their programming services or have a kickback (finders-fee) arrangement with hardware vendors.

Many of the large "establishment" consulting firms have large fees and elaborate procedures that are basically the same as the procedures used when computer systems and vendors were untried and systems cost $1 million. Some cynics think that the prices of the systems consultants recommend are reflected in their fees.

The primary roles of computer consultants are to help design and find (or improve the existing system to become) the best system for your unique business and to bridge the communication gap between you and the programming technicians. The consultant must understand your business and your unique methods of operation. Most computer consultants have only a programming and technical background. They fail to understand that business management is much more than just (lots of) computer reports.

When you select a consultant in any field, make sure he is truly independent, and, most importantly, make sure that he understands your business and personal method of operation, and that he communicates well with you.

Many customers look to their CPA for computer consulting

services. A Certified Public Accountant is a person licensed to certify financial statements. That is all. Certification of financial statements may be required by investors or lenders and, in the case of publicly held companies, is required by the government. This certification states that the financial statements were audited and prepared according to certain standards. Qualifying for a CPA license requires education, experience, and passing an exam in relation to auditing and certifying statements.

A CPA license does not require competence or experience in the areas of preparing tax returns, preparing management information reports, or computer or other consulting. A CPA, however, signs a pledge to not undertake any professional activity in which he is not professionally competent. This pledge is self-judged and self-administered.

A CPA also pledges to maintain independence (or disclose to the client the nature of his relevant associations) and to maintain confidentiality of client records. This section of the code can be and is enforced. CPAs have lost their licenses for violations.

When you retain a CPA for tax work, management information, or computer or other consulting, it is "let the buyer beware," because there can be widely varying degrees of competence. These activities do not require a CPA or any other license, and you will find individuals without any license more qualified for these activities than some CPAs. Using a licensed CPA, however, will give you reasonably good assurance that your information will be treated professionally and confidentially and that the CPA is not receiving undisclosed kickbacks in relation to the work performed.

Many professional accountants give their clients improper advice concerning computers. This is not too surprising, since most accountants (including CPAs) are about on a par with the rest of the small businesses in not effectively utilizing modern computers to reduce costs and improve service. (There is a big difference between effectively utilizing a computer and using [or having] a computer.) You can tell that your accountant is effectively utilizing modern computer capabilities if: (a) you are getting "management information" in addition to financial statements and tax returns; (b) you are receiving this information on a timely basis (within two weeks after the financial statements' date); and (c) your accounting fees have decreased over the last three years.

(If you obtain your own computer, what will happen to your accountant's fees?)

Management information, in addition to financial statements, is product/product-line, customer/territory/region, unit price/cost, inventory, percentage/ratio, comparative (to budget, last year, or beginning of year), transaction backup, etc., reporting and analysis. Most importantly, management information must be custom designed for each business's management. These are the types of things that a computer does best—and faster and at less cost.

Furthermore, many accountants tend to be somewhat conservative in that they avoid risks or potential mistakes. (The best way to avoid mistakes is to do nothing or, failing that, not to make any changes.) Since everyone has heard some of the computer "horror" stories, avoiding computers seems to be a nice "safe" approach. But stagnation in a competitive, changing world is never really safe.

Professional, independent computer consultants do not represent any brand or receive any commissions or fees from the sellers. They do not program and are, therefore, not selling a programming service tied into a hardware brand. They should view hundreds of computer systems in operation each year, make numerous reference checks each week, and do substantial research. Each year they should be involved in over $1 million worth of computer hardware and software decisions and problems involving a wide variety of hardware brands, local dealers, software vendors and computer services.

Obviously, quality work in this area increases with quantity because it generates experience and leverage with vendors. In order to maintain independence, fees must be paid by the client, but, because of experience and volume, these fees should be nominal and more than offset by substantial reductions in the cost of a working system. A good consultant is a helper and advisor who is on your side.

The best way to establish a strong working relationship with a consultant or advisor is to have this person prepare an initial study with defined objectives at an agreed-upon total price. This should be payable after completion of the job to your satisfaction. A professional, like a doctor or lawyer, does not require a contract for professional services.

	$4,000 SYSTEM		$20,000 SYSTEM		$100,000 SYSTEM	
	AMOUNT	PERCENT SYSTEM COST	AMOUNT	PERCENT SYSTEM COST	AMOUNT	PERCENT SYSTEM COST
1. Two- to three-hour review and two- to four-page report on benefits, estimated cost, including potential systems and vendors	$200	5.0%	$ 300	1.5%	$ 500	0.5%
2. Preparation of system requirements, feasibility analysis, and requests for proposals	400	10.0	1,200	6.0	2,500	2.5
3. Mailings to vendors; vendor discussions, reference checks, on-site evaluations, and recommendation (ranking)	(Not applicable for off-the-shelf systems, as buyer must self-test)		1,200	6.0	2,000	2.0
4. Contract review and recommendations, review of specifications, and implementation progress reviews	(Not cost justified for smaller systems)				1,500	1.5
TOTAL	$600	15.0%	$2,700	13.5%	$6,500	6.5%

FIGURE 14–1 Computer Consulting Guidelines

Extensive contracts and proposals are expensive and must be reflected in the price of the contracted service. Consulting contracts are supposed to protect both the consultant and the client; however, they usually favor the consultant. The contract is also supposed to specify what the client will receive; however, the client usually retains a consultant because the client is not an expert and does not know what to expect. The consultant should be the expert and create useable results and products that increase the client's knowledge and understanding of the project. A good consultant can provide these services effectively without the unnecessary costs of a contract. The consultant, however, may issue a brief letter or fee schedule outlining the services with not-to-exceed fee quotes. Services should be on a satisfaction-guaranteed basis and paid as the service products are completed.

An initial consulting review costing $200 to $500 may be of use to the client in becoming acquainted with the consultant and his capabilities. The first major use of a consultant is in preparing the system requirements, as described in Chapter 11. A professionally prepared systems requirements document will provide a valuable analysis of the business and will serve as the basis for a feasibility analysis of the proposed computer investment. This document and analysis will be valuable for business planning even if the computer project is discontinued or deferred. A good consultant, because of experience and up-to-date knowledge of sources, will be able to efficiently select vendors to evaluate and then complete evaluations. For larger systems, the consultant will be a valuable advisor for the contract review, system equipment and software item analysis (so that the client does not pay too much or get unnecessary expensive items or features), and implementation monitoring. Some guidelines for the cost of these services are shown in Fig. 14–1.

Quality professional advice and management are not expensive, as they will more than pay for themselves. The alternative may be very expensive.

15

CONCLUSION: PROFITABLE COMPUTING

The purpose of a computer in business is to provide top management with easy-to-read, accurate, clear, concise, and timely information that is conducive to action. Clerical effort required for input must be minimized and be easy to supervise and control.

The basic accounting system should be effectively and efficiently functioning before implementing a computer system. More sophisticated systems must operate from a solid base. Many small to medium-sized companies or profit centers do not need sophisticated systems; a good, solid, basic system may eliminate the previously apparent need for an excessively complex system. The basic accounting system builds a foundation that can be expanded. More systems can be modularly added as the organization changes and the information requirements and desires change. Basic and modular systems that are implemented must facilitate changes.

The first goal of a computer system or service is to improve the effectiveness of all members of the organization via better accounting activities and financial management information. First, the president, general manager, or functional manager must not wade through details and make decisions with uncertainty surrounding the accuracy and completeness of the information he is using. He should be making forward-moving decisions based on correct information received on a timely basis. Second, the controller or accounting manager must not spend the majority of his time supervising and checking the generation of voluminous detail. Rather, he should spend most of his efforts analyzing summary reports and, when the summary information indicates the need, request and/or analyze more detailed information. He should present requested and selected information along with interpretations and recommendations. Third, the clerical staff should not be overwhelmed with repetitive, menial tasks that are best suited for the computer. They should be operating the computer and preparing special analyses to assist the controller.

The current technology can accomplish these goals for the business organization. Details must be maintained and controlled, but should not be routinely presented to all levels of management. Current computer hardware is so powerful, that poorly designed software can generate a proliferation of management information that, many times, makes the information difficult to use for the busy executive. On the other hand, current computers have tremendous capabilities to summarize data and present concise, comparative-type reports, as compared to forests that obscure the trees. Presentation of summary and/or exceptional information can highlight areas needing action or further review. Summary information can be functionally customized to fit various management needs throughout the organization.

Small, single-user computers called personal computers are having an increasingly important role in business organizations for increasing professional and clerical productivity. These computers should more properly be called professional computers. They provide an extremely useful, low-cost tool for the professional who needs to analyze data or maintain and update documents that do not pertain to the voluminous accounting and detailed transaction records of the business.

Technology and increased productivity, whether computers, printing presses, other tools, or energy, have never in history eliminated or reduced jobs. They have only changed jobs, increased total jobs, created a greater variety of jobs, and improved working and living conditions. Increased productivity reduces poverty, increases life expectancy, and increases individual freedom through increased choices available to satisfy individual styles and preferences.

Every member of society, especially every professional and

business manager, has a great deal that needs to be accomplished. We need to use all of the tools available to us, including the modern computer technology.

Proper use of computers or computer services in a business will make everyone's job easier and more fulfilling, along with increasing the business' profitability. Mistakes, however, will be very disruptive and expensive.

The maze of hardware and software capabilities and combinations currently available can make the computer system decision very difficult and complex. Computerization is a complex and critical project. Good project management procedures that have been covered in this book are the key to success.

Computer hardware technology has rapidly advanced, and very powerful equipment is now available at a low cost. Software development has considerably lagged behind the development of hardware capability. The development of trained, skilled personnel to utilize and manage the software and hardware is considerably behind both the hardware and software. Software, personnel support, and training are now the critical factors in computer systems evaluation and selection. Software evaluation requires the combined efforts of skilled professionals in business management, controllership, accounting, and data processing.

The key points to remember are: (1) when purchasing a computer or changing an existing system, specify and buy the software before the hardware; (2) the people from whom you buy are much more important than the brand; (3) much of the advice and information you will receive from publications and so-called experts is out of date, erroneous, or influenced by advertisers or other special interests; (4) information and advice should be sought, but it should be questioned and, when used, used carefully; and (5) when undertaking any endeavor of this type, the best investments you can make are in education, preparation, specification, documentation, and caution.

Computers are a tremendous productivity tool. The businesses that know best how to use computers effectively have a tremendous advantage over their competitors. Computers offer a tremendous challenge and opportunity for all professionals and managers to increase the productivity of our scarce and skilled human resources.

APPENDIX 1: GLOSSARY
APPENDIX 2: HARDWARE
BRANDS AND SYSTEMS

APPENDICES

GLOSSARY

Acoustic Coupler Telephone connecting device used to link computers and/or computer peripherals.

Analog Computer Computer that does processing by means of continuous, rather than discrete, logic.

Application Software Programs for users that are dedicated to a specific purpose, e.g., payroll.

ASCII Data format for the representation of characters promulgated by the American Standards Code for Information Interchange.

Background Computer activity that is not apparent to the user.

Backup Copy of information or data used just in case original is lost.

Band Printer Line printer.

Bar Code Reader Device to read standard bars representing numbers.

BASIC A computer language.

Baud Bits per second (unit of transmission of information).

Beta Site One of first system installation sites.

Binary Having two elements; characteristic of digital computers.

Bit Binary digit.

Bubble Memory Memory comprised of a thin film of magnetic material in which discrete "bubbles" of polarity opposite from that of the main material reside.

Buffer Temporary data storage space within a computer or peripheral.

Bus Line of communication in a computer.

Byte Eight bits, one standard character.

Cards, Punched Data medium, now essentially obsolete, on which punched holes, in various rows and columns, represent information.

Cathode Ray Tube (CRT) Television-type screen used for inputting and viewing computer information.

Central Processing Unit (CPU) Controlling and arithmetic/logic unit of a computer system.

Chain Printer Line printer.

Characters per second (cps) A speed of transmission of information to a computer printer or terminal.

Character Printer Printer that prints characters sequentially.

Chip Small electronic device made of silicon that houses a complex, microscopic circuit.

COBOL A computer language.

Communication Exchange of information among computers.

Compiler Computer program to translate instructions in a high-level computer language to a series of binary digits that is machine-acceptable.

Computer System of circuitry and related devices given over to the task of processing information.

Computer System Computer plus all devices and software required for the processing of information.

Controller Computer within the computer designed to control the operation of the system.

Core CPU memory.

Coupler, Acoustic See Acoustic Coupler.

CP/M Single-user computer operating system.

cps Characters per second; a rate of transmission of information.

CPU See Central Processing Unit.

CPU Memory Information stored internally and immediately accessible to the CPU.

CRT See Cathode Ray Tube.

Daisywheel Mechanism by means of which letter-quality characters may be produced by a printer.

Data Information used by a computer program. Sometimes held to be the program as well.

Data Base Management System (DBMS) System for maintaining and manipulating a large amount of information usually required for generating reports for management.

Data Processing (DP) Synonym for computing or computer, i. e., the DP department is the computer department.

DBMS See Data Base Management System.

Dealer A seller to end users.

Desk-top Computer A compact computer system deriving its name from the ease with which it is said to fit on a desk.

Digital Pertaining to discrete elements.

Digital Computer Computer that does processing by means of discrete, rather than continuous, logic.

Disk A flat, thin plate for storing computer data.

Disk Drive A device for reading and recording disk data.

Disk Operating System (DOS) Operating system for a disk-oriented computer.

Diskettes Very thin, flexible disks.

Distributed Data Processing Data processing performed by a network of computers linked together in such manner that they are able to communicate with one another.

Distributor A seller to dealers.

DOS See Disk Operating System.

Dot Matrix A grid wherein various points are lighted to present characters to the viewer of a CRT or similar device. Also a type of printer that forms letters using a dot grid.

DP See Data Processing.

Drive (Disk) See Disk Drive.

EDP Electronic Data Processing. See Data Processing.

Electronic Data Processing (EDP) See Data Processing.

Electronic Spreadsheet A package for computer-aided data tables.

File A data set that contains all records of a given type.

File Management System Internal computer system for arranging data files so that the user may easily understand them.

Firmware Programs permanently imbedded in electronic chips.

Floppy Disks See Diskettes.

Foreground Computer activity that is apparent to the user.

FORTRAN A computer language.

GIGO Acronym for "Garbage in, Garbage Out."

Graphics Plots or charts of data.

Hard Copy Information printed on paper or the like, as distinguished from information written on a CRT or the like.

Hard Disk Medium for the storage of data in a rigid, nonflexible form.

Hardware Computer equipment and peripherals.

Information See Data.

Input Data entered into the computer.

Integrators (Systems) See Systems Integrators.

I/O Input/Output.

K Thousand, as in 35 K bytes of memory.

KISS Acronym for "Keep It Simple, Stupid."

Language Dictionary of terms and rules, with definitions on how they are interpreted by the computer's operating system.

Large-Scale Integration (LSI) Logic of a chip with a complex circuitry.

Letter-Quality Printers Printers whose type is of the quality of typewriters.

Line Printers Printers that print an entire line at a time.

Lines per minute (lpm) Speed at which a line printer prints.

lpm See Lines per minute.

LSI See Large-Scale Integration.

M Million, as in 2 M bytes of memory.

Magnetic Tape Medium for storing computer data.

Mainframe Large and very powerful computer to which many users are simultaneously connected.

Mass Storage Storage external to the computer on which a large amount of data can be located; usually disk or tape storage.

Matrix See Dot Matrix.

MB See Megabyte.

Medium (pl., media) Device, such as a tape or disk, on which information is recorded.

Megabyte (MB) Million bytes.

Memory Information stored either internally in the computer or on some external medium such as disk or tape.

Menu Set of options, usually in an applications software package, that is displayed in tabular form on a keyboard or CRT screen.

Metal Oxide Semiconductor (MOS) Technology for making LSI chips.

Microcomputer Small computer, usually for personal, dedicated (including robotics) or small-business use.

Microprocessor CPU on a chip, used in microcomputers.

Minicomputer Medium-sized computer, with capabilities in between those of large mainframes and microcomputers.

Modem Signal converter to which a telephone that communicates with a computer is attached.

MOS See Metal Oxide Semiconductor.

MP/M A multiuser computer operating system.

Multiuser Pertaining to the simultaneous computer processing of information by users.

Multitasking Simultaneous computer processing of many tasks.

Multiprogramming Simultaneous computer processing of many programs.

OASIS A multiuser DBMS computer operating system.

OCR See Optical Character Recognition.

OEM See Original Equipment Manufacturer.

Off-line Stored externally to the computer.

On-line Stored internally in the computer for ready access.

Operating System (OS) Set of computer instructions for running software and data.

Optical Character Recognition (OCR) Means of converting typed copy into electronic data for subsequent computer processing.

Original Equipment Manufacturer (OEM) Assembler of computer equipment components that have been manufactured by others.

OS See Operating System.

Output Information displayed or printed by the computer.

Package Software program that can be purchased, usually for a given application.

Paper Tape Obsolete rolls of paper used for data.

Parallel Pertaining to the simultaneous transmission and/or processing of many blocks of data.

Parameter A variable inserted to customize an application software package.

PASCAL A computer language.

Password Individual identification by means of which user information is protected and private.

PCM See Plug-compatible Mainframe.

Peripherals Devices and equipment connected to the central computer unit.

Personal Computer Single-user, limited-capability computer, usually a microcomputer.

Plug-compatible Mainframe (PCM) Non-IBM mainframe that can replace an IBM mainframe with no change in software.

Port I/O plug into the computer.

Printer Device for printing computer output.

Program Set of computer instructions for processing data.

PROM Programmable Read-only Memory; see Read-only Memory.

Punched Cards See Cards, Punched.

RAM See Random-access Memory.

Random-access Memory (RAM) CPU memory that can be randomly accessed and revised.

Read-only Memory (ROM) CPU memory that can be accessed but not easily revised.

Record All information for one and the same item.

Remote Job Entry (RJE) Remote entry and collection of computer data and results.

Request for Proposals (RFP) Request for preliminary quotes and specifications from vendors.

RFP See Request for Proposals.

RJE See Remote Job Entry.

ROM See Read-only Memory.

RPG A computer language.

RS-232 Standard I/O specification.

S-100 Standard microcomputer internal bus.

Selectric A type of IBM character typewriter or printer.

Serial Pertaining to the sequential transmission and/or processing of single elements or digits of data.

Small-business Computers Computers in businesses without a DP department.

Soft Copy Information on a CRT screen, as distinguished from information printed on paper.

Software Set of programs or instructions designed to perform a computer task.

Spooling Storing data to be printed.

Storage Memory, either internal to the computer, or external to it, in the form of disk or tape.

System See Computer System.

Systems House See Systems Integrator.

Systems Integrator A seller of systems built out of components from different manufacturers.

Tape See Magnetic Tape.

Terminal TV-type screen and keyboard; see CRT.

Thimble Print element for a character printer.

Turnkey System Computer system that processes data when the system is accepted by the purchaser.

Turnkey Vendor Seller of turnkey systems.

UNIX Computer operating system designed for scientific calculations.

Variable-length Records Records stored in a format that makes efficient use of computer storage space.

VDT See Video Display Tube; same as CRT.

Video Display Tube (VDT) Input terminal; see CRT.

Virtual Memory Operating system technique for rapidly moving data and programs in and out of CPU memory.

Wafer A thin disk of electronic material used for computer circuitry.

Winchester Hermetically sealed hard-disk unit.

Word Processing Package or system designed to manipulate text.

Word Size Number of bits in the word image that the computer recognizes.

XENIX A microcomputer version of UNIX.

APPENDIX 2

HARDWARE BRANDS AND SYSTEMS

USER RATINGS

Datapro (publisher of a research service for computer professionals) conducts an extensive survey of computer users. The survey results should be used with caution. The users surveyed are obtained from *Computerworld* subscription lists; however, the most successful small-business computer systems are well supported by the vendor, so that the user of these systems probably does not subscribe to or read *Computerworld*. Many purchasers are not aware that they could have received much more for what they paid. Many purchasers are reluctant to admit that they have made mistakes.

The results of a recent survey for small-business computer and minicomputer manufacturers are given in Table A2–1. The twenty-two companies that received more than 6 valid responses (out of 2753) are listed. The number of responses for each manufacturer is indicative of the popularity of the manufacturer among users with data processing departments (*Computerworld* readers).

SYSTEM SPEEDS

The Association of Computer Users (ACU, P.O. Box 9003, Boulder, Colorado 80301) conducts benchmark tests on numerous computer systems. The results shown in Table A2–2 for small com-

212

Table A2–1
SMALL-BUSINESS COMPUTERS AND MINICOMPUTERS, DATAPRO USER RATINGS, JUNE 1982

OVERALL SATISFACTION RANK, COMPANY	SCORE*	NUMBER**
1. Point 4	3.63	8
2. Hewlett Packard	3.50	226
3. Tandem	3.42	25
4. Microdata (McDonnell Douglas)	3.37	43
5. Prime	3.36	84
6. Wang	3.36	87
7. IBM	3.34	1172
8. DEC	3.31	332
9. Texas Instruments	3.29	32
10. Burroughs	3.18	231
11. Qantel (Mohawk)	3.17	6
12. NCR	3.16	49
13. Honeywell	3.14	37
14. Datapoint	3.11	66
15. Basic Four (MAI)	3.07	44
16. Data General	2.98	131
17. (All Others)	2.97	72
18. Four-Phase	2.84	51
19. Sperry Univac	2.67	6
20. Harris	2.63	16
21. Perkin-Elmer	2.61	24
22. General Automation	2.45	11

*4 = Excellent, 3 = Good, 2 = Fair, 1 = Poor. Average, e.g., 3.63.
**Replies in survey, e.g., 8.

puters, along with narrative discussions by Hillel Segal, ACU president, were published in the May 17, 1982 and June 28, 1982 issues of *Computerworld*. The complete reports are available from the ACU at the above address.

The reports and articles include numerous caveats on the use of these test results. Software has a major impact on the speed at which a given application will be completed. Each system has unique characteristics, and different programming will affect the running-time efficiency. One system may process an application

Table A2–2
BENCHMARK TESTS OF 25 SMALL COMPUTERS*

ACCOUNTS RECEIVABLE RANK, SYSTEM	TEST TIME (min)		SYSTEM PRICE
	ACCOUNTS RECEIVABLE	SCIENTIFIC ENGINEERING	
1. Altos ACS8000-6 (Hard Disk)	1:35.1	7:54.5	$12,340
2. Smoke Signal Chieftain 9822	1:40.7	3:13.3	8,149
3. North Star Horizon	1:57.7	12:01.9	6,911
4. Wang 2200 SVP	2:23.0	2:13.3	14,600
5. Vector Graphic 3005	2:26.9	11:34.1	11,150
6. Data General CS/10 (Hard Disk)	2:40.3	58:21.0	15,500
7. Cromemco System Two	2:48.0	14:52.6	9,275
8. Alpha Micro AM-1011	3:25.3	5:18.3	15,605
9. Digital Microsystems DSC-2	3:28.8	13:24.9	9,085
10. Commodore CBM-8032	3:36.0	23:45.1	4,085
11. Texas Instruments 771	3:38.1	22:05.4	12,100
12. Radio Shack TRS-80-II	3:38.6	20:00.7	7,648
13. Altos ACS 8000-15	3:52.7	5:39.3	8,875
14. IBM 5120	4:16.2	35:29.7	13,705
15. Decstation 78	4:21.5	7:55.7	11,570
16. Dynabyte 5300	4:38.0	5:39.5	7,835
17. Billings BC-12 DF2M	5:09.2	21:48.6	11,395
18. NEC Astra 205	5:10.8	14:27.9	9,890
19. Xerox 820	5:30.1	24:37.0	7,220
20. Vector Graphic System B	5:56.5	19:30.0	7,750
21. Pertec PCC 2000	6:04.3	28:48.4	12,270
22. SD Systems SD-200	6:16.4	17:42.8	12,300
23. Apple II+	6:17.4	21:11.0	4,270
24. IBM Personal Computer	9:21.8	17:29.6	4,550
25. Ohio Scientific C3-A	15:49.3	12:10.7	10,440
Average	4:22.6	16:49.4	$ 9,941

*As published in May 17, 1982 and June 28, 1982 issues of *Computerworld*. By Hillel Segal, President, Association of Computer Users, P.O. Box 9003, Boulder, CO 80301. CW Communications/Inc. Framingham, MA 01701–Reprinted from *Computerworld*.

faster than another system with a certain programming design; however, the results might be reversed with another programming design.

These test results are useful in providing insight into the relative performance of various systems. The best evaluation criterion is to see applications similar to yours in operation at a customer site using the programs (or programs from the programmer) you are evaluating.

The accounts receivable problem creates a file of fifty records that is randomly updated ten times. Sales and payment information are generated. This type of problem requires considerable disk-to-memory data transfer and is typical of most business applications. Time on the test is used for the performance ranking.

The scientific/engineering problem is not typical of most business applications. This problem tests the computers' speeds for processing complex mathematical problems in the CPU memory. The test problem solves a system of linear equations with fifty variables and fifty unknowns and uses the Gauss-Jordan method of elimination. The 16-bit computers generally performed best on this type of problem.

There is a wide variation in performance among the systems tested, yielding no correlation between price and performance. The Smoke Signal Chieftain and North Star Horizon show the best performance-to-price ratio for floppy disk systems. The Altos ACS-8000-6 shows good performance for a low-cost hard-disk system. The Commodore CBM-8032 at $4,085 was the lowest price system tested; its price was less than half the average, but its performance was above average. The popular Apple II + and IBM Personal Computers showed slow performance on the business application test.

The most significant thing to come out of these benchmark test results is that there is a tremendous range of computer processing speeds and no correlation between price and performance. The 16-bit machines are not necessarily faster than 8-bit machines for accounting applications. For the scientific application, the fastest machine, Wang 2200SVP, was twenty-six times faster than the slowest machine, Data General CS/10; and the slower machine cost more.

SYSTEM SPECIFICATIONS

A summary of some popular small-business computer systems is shown in Tables A2–3 to A2–7. It includes four typical configurations and the approximate price of each system. Most of the information was obtained via direct replies from the manufacturers in response to a survey requesting the tabulated information. Some manufacturers did not reply, and, in these cases, information was obtained from published sources and local dealers.

Considerable care was exercised in obtaining, analyzing and tabulating the data; however, because of numerous sources and rapid changes in the industry, the accuracy cannot be guaranteed. Prices will vary according to vendor pricing policies. When a system is being considered, current price quotes, features, and specifications should be obtained from the potential supplying vendor.

HOW TO USE SYSTEM SPECIFICATIONS

When considering potential computer hardware systems, you should first determine the number of terminals and printers you will initially require. You should then estimate your potential needs in two to three years. The total number of printers and terminals is the number of I/O (Input/Output) ports required.

If you initially need just a single-user system and are not doing business accounting, a floppy disk system may be all that is required. A dual floppy disk system is considered the minimum system to be of productive use in business. This is so because two diskettes are the minimum configuration for backing up and transferring data between internal data bases. (The exception to this rule would be where there is a central dual-diskette machine readily available for backing up and data transfer. Dispersed users may then have their own single-diskette computers.)

If a computer is to be used for the management of a business, a hard-disk system will probably be required—certainly if interrelated information currently requires more than one-fourth of one file drawer. An example is all the business' accounting plus either customers, vendors, inventory, or payroll. A data base management system for more than 500 items plus activity will also usually require a hard-disk system.

After the minimum and expansion requirements have been determined, you should review the "System Summaries Approximate End-User Prices" by manufacturer (Table A2–3). This summary lists systems' prices and maximum expansion for the software and hardware brand as published by Easy Data Corporation in March, 1983. As a starting point you should select the systems with the minimum price for the initial and potential configurations. (Current summaries and specifications for all listed systems are available from Easy Data Corporation, 1600 Dove Street, Suite 338, Newport Beach, CA 92660, tel. (714)851–8148.)

The next step is to compare features for the selected systems. Features for a few selected systems as of March, 1983 are shown in Table A2–4 for single-user floppy disk systems; Table A2–5 for single-user hard-disk systems; Table A2–6 for four-user, two-printer systems; and Table A2–7 for ten-user, three-printer systems. Additional descriptions of the table features follow.

Systems' prices, specifications, and features change rapidly. Current prices, specifications, and features should be obtained from potential suppliers. The information requested should be in a format that facilitates easy comparisons. It can then be compared against that furnished by the computer vendors, that published here, and that published in current periodicals and research publications.

There are wide variations for quotes from different manufacturers for specified configurations and features. There are wide variations in available features among the brands. A potential purchaser should evaluate the prices and features and determine his features and capability needs versus cost. The tabulated configurations provide a good starting point for comparing systems. From the specified data and prices of peripherals, it is relatively easy to estimate prices of systems configured in between the listed configurations or increased from the maximum listed configurations.

Manufacturers' addresses and phone numbers are listed at the conclusion of this Appendix. The manufacturers can provide you the names of their best vendors in your area.

PRICES AND FEATURES

Following are a description and related information regarding the features of the more popular small-business computers.

1. **Prices.** See the requested specifications for each of the four configurations. The following specifications are for the system quoted.
2. **Word Size.** CPU word size in bits.

3. **CPU Memory.** K bytes of RAM memory.
4. **Disk, on-line.** MB on-line and accessible by CPU RAM.
5. **Backup.** MB on a single item of the backup medium (i.e., floppy disk, disk or tape cartridge, etc.).
6. **Backup Type.** DISK-disk cartridge or pack, FLPY-Floppy Diskette, TAPE-Tape cassette or reel, VCR-Video Cassette Recorder.
7. **Printers.** cps or lpm speeds of the printers included in the quote.
8. **PTRs and CRTs Supplied by Same.** Are the quoted printers and CRTs, respectively, supplied by the computer system manufacturer?
9. **Screen Size.** Diagonal measurement in inches/number of characters. The industry standard is 12 inches and 1920 characters (80 by 24 rows), and this is designated by 12/1920.
10. **Maximum Upgrade.** From the same manufacturer, the maximum system that the user can upgrade to and still use all software previously used on the quoted system. (Number of ports is the maximum number of printers, terminals, and other communication lines that can independently access the central computer.)
11. **Features.** Are the following software and features available on the quoted system?

    A. CP/M.   CP/M operating system and packages.

    B. MP/M.   MP/M operating system and packages

    C. Unix or Xenix.   Either of these operating systems.

    D. OASIS.   OASIS operating system.

    E. BASIC.   BASIC programming language.

    F. Word Processing.   Word processing software.

    G. DBMS.   Data base management software.

    H. Accounting.   Accounting applications programs (packages).

    I. Simultaneous File Access.   Two or more users may simultaneously access the same information in the computer on-line disk file.

    J. CRT Multitasking.   Two jobs can be simultaneously processed on a single CRT.

    K. Spooling.   CRT can be used for one job while the printer is printing another job.

    L. RS–232 Peripherals.   Can industry-standard peripherals be plugged into the system?

    M. Unlimited (Shared) System.   Networking system where each CRT contains an individual CPU (and possibly mass storage). The central computer simply directs communication; when a CRT is not accessing the central or another CRT's mass storage file (disk) or printer, its operation does not affect the central computer or any other CRT.

> **N.** Software Included. Are the application (word processing, DBMS, and accounting) software packages included in the quoted price?

SYSTEM CONFIGURATIONS

The manufacturers were asked to quote systems that come as close as possible to the specifications given below for each configuration. Where the manufacturer does not supply the peripherals, the indicated prices for standard RS–232 peripherals were used. Where the peripherals are included in a package cost for a base configuration, the add-on costs were used and subtracted from the CPU/disk unit cost; a user can use these unit costs as add-ons to estimate the cost of a system with more peripherals.

1. Single-user floppy disk system.
    A. Diskette drives: two minimum capacity.
    B. Terminal: minimum. (If not supplied by manufacturer, use RS–232 standard at $800.)
    C. Printer: 80 position, 80 cps. (If not supplied by manufacturer, use RS–232 standard at $800.)
2. Single-user hard-disk system.
    A. Hard disk: minimum available, but greater than 5MB.
    B. Backup: minimum cost.
    C. Terminal: limited intelligence and features. (If not supplied by manufacturer, use RS–232 standard at $900.)
    D. Printer: dot-matrix, 132 position, 150 cps. (If not supplied by manufacturer, use RS–232 standard at $1,800.)
3. Four-user, two-printer system.
    A. Hard disk: 20 to 50MB.
    B. Backup: fifty to one hundred percent of the on-line capacity, if available.
    C. Terminals: four, with some intelligence and features. (If not supplied by manufacturer, use RS–232 standard at $1,000 each, total $4,000.)
    D. Printers: 1) dot-matrix, 132 position, 150 cps; 2) letter quality, 40 cps. (If not supplied by manufacturer, use RS–232 standard at $1,800 and $2,500, respectively; total $4,300.)
4. Ten-user, three-printer system.
    A. Hard disk: 70 to 100MB.

B. Backup: 50 to 100 percent of the on-line capacity, if available.

C. Terminals: ten, with intelligence and features. (If not supplied by manufacturer, use RS–232 standard at $1,000 each, total $10,000.)

D. Printers: 1) dot-matrix, 132 position, 150 cps; 2) letter quality, 40 cps; 3) dot-matrix, 300 lpm. (If not supplied by manufacturer, use RS–232 standard at $1,800, $2,500, and $6,500, respectively; total $10,800.)

Table A2–3
EASY DATA COMPUTER COMPARISONS
SYSTEMS SUMMARIES: END-USER PRICES

MANUFACTURER	YEAR ESTAB-LISHED	ANNUAL DP REVENUE (MILLIONS)	MAXIMUM I/Os	ONE-USER FLOPPY DISK SYSTEM	ONE USER, 5+ MB HARD DISK	4 USERS, 20+ MB 2 PRINTERS	10 USERS, 70+ MB 3 PRINTERS
Access Matrix Corp.	1982	$ 1	6	$ 2,500*	$ 9,700	$ 25,000	$ 47,400
Action Computer	1978	1	150				
ADDS (Applied Dig. Data Sys.)	1969	50					
Multivision			6	5,400	8,800	35,100	65,800
Mentor			34		28,800	29,100	47,800
Alpha Micro Systems	1977	27	68		11,200		
Alspa	1981	1	3	3,800	10,100		
Altos Computer	1977	65					
8 Bit			7	4,600	8,700		
16 Bit			17		17,700	25,300	39,800
Apple Computer	1977	710					
IIe			2	3,300			
III			2	5,100	6,700		
Lisa			2	10,700	13,000		
Archives, Inc	1978	4	2	6,300			
Ardent Computer Prod.	1980	3	16		12,500	27,400	43,400
Atari	1972	200	2	3,900			
ATV Jacquard	1969	112	62	15,400**	21,400	49,000	94,200
Barrington International	1980	1	2		10,700		
Basic Four (MAI)	1971	360	64	5,500	10,000	39,000	123,500
Beehive International	1968	40	3	3,800			
Billings Computer	1976	10	9,999	3,100	6,300	25,500	51,500
Blackhawk Computer	1979	1	16	5,300	8,800	20,500	37,800
BMC Systems, Inc.	1976	8	5	4,700	11,000		

Table A2–3 (continued)

MANUFACTURER	YEAR ESTABLISHED	ANNUAL DP REVENUE (MILLIONS)	MAXIMUM I/Os	ONE-USER FLOPPY DISK SYSTEM	ONE USER, 5+ MB HARD DISK	4 USERS, 20+ MB 2 PRINTERS	10 USERS, 70+ MB 3 PRINTERS
BTI Computer Systems	1968	25	32		42,400	47,600	64,200
Burr-Brown Research	1956	5	8	8,900			
Burroughs Corporation	1885	3,700	9,999				
B–20 Series			16	8,400	12,400	38,300	74,800
B–90 Series			8	8,400	24,200	42,300	
B–900 Series			36			48,600	91,000
Bytronix Corp.	1977	4	6		12,500	21,700	
CADO Systems Corp.	1973	85	8	9,000	13,500	32,500	
Canon U.S.A., Inc.	1966	20	2	4,100			
CAPRO Inc.	1980	2	42		42,600	49,800	74,400
Casio Inc.	1970	1	2	3,000			
Centurion Computer (EDS)	1971	15	32		18,500	45,900	94,500
Century Computer	1975	2	20		19,800	31,000	57,800
Challenge Systems	1982	1	2	5,800			
Chromatics, Inc.	1976	8	3	8,300	27,800		
CIE Systems	1981	20	32	8,300	8,600		
Codata	1978	4	18		15,600	22,700	47,000
CODEX (Motorola)	1962	50	2	5,800		29,200	48,200
Colonial Data Services	1980	1	4	5,600	11,400		
Columbia Data Prod.	1976	10	5	4,800	8,200		
Commodore Business Mach.	1976	455	5	3,600	7,800		
Compal, Inc.	1976	4					
Electric Briefcase			2	2,800	6,800		
EZ Type			2	6,500	11,200		
8200			60	7,500	11,300	31,000	
Comptek Research	1968	11	8		26,100	60,000	

MANUFACTURER	YEAR ESTAB-LISHED	ANNUAL DP REVENUE (MILLIONS)	MAXIMUM I/Os	ONE-USER FLOPPY DISK SYSTEM	ONE USER, 5+ MB HARD DISK	4 USERS, 20+ MB 2 PRINTERS	10 USERS, 70+ MB 3 PRINTERS
Compucorp	1969	20	4	8,700	13,400		
CompuPro Systems	1974	5	16	6,600	11,700		
Computer Automation	1975	83	32		34,200	41,500	66,800
Computer Devices	1969	20	8	4,600			
Computer Talk	1972	1	256	6,800	32,100	50,200	100,600
Convergent Technology	1979	25	16		20,000	40,000	
Corvus	1979	28	64		9,300	25,200	64,700
CPT Corporation	1971	180	9	10,000	19,000	43,000	
Cromemco, Inc.	1975	77	18	6,600	18,500	33,400	
Cybersystems, Inc.	1974	3	2	7,000	11,100		
Data General	1968	760					
MPT/100			8	7,700	14,400	31,500	
Nova/Eclipse			64		16,300	37,600	92,900
Data Systems Marketing	1970	20	4	3,800			
Data Technology	1976	10	11	5,100	7,800	17,100*	
Datamac Corporation	1960	1	3	5,000	9,300		
Datapoint Corp.	1968	474					
1800 Series			9	9,800	25,200	41,900	
ARC Network			9,999		34,200	41,900	84,700
Datavue Corporation	1971	5	10	4,100	9,400	26,900	
DEC (Digital Equipment Corp.)	1957	4,000	9,999				
Rainbow			2	4,500	9,800		
Professional			2	5,000	10,300		
DECmate			2	3,900	11,500		
PDP 11			127		24,000	34,700	112,900
Delta Data Systems	1968	24	33	7,200	14,500	27,300	58,800

Table A2–3 (continued)

MANUFACTURER	YEAR ESTAB-LISHED	ANNUAL DP REVENUE (MILLIONS)	MAXIMUM I/Os	ONE-USER FLOPPY DISK SYSTEM	ONE USER, 5+ MB HARD DISK	4 USERS, 20+ MB 2 PRINTERS	10 USERS, 70+ MB 3 PRINTERS
Digital Computer Corp.	1978	2	32	5,100	9,000	22,300	45,800
Digital Microsystems	1968	10	9,999	4,800	9,300	32,300	81,300
Digital Systems Corp.	1975	8	15		42,600	52,600	
Distributed Computer Systems	1975	2	2	5,700			
Durango Systems	1977	20	4	12,000	20,000		
Dynabyte	1977	10	18	8,600	14,700	23,300	45,800
E & H Electronics	1977	1	60	6,700	14,500	29,500	
Eagle Computer	1981	1	11	3,800	7,800	23,300	
Epic Computer Corp.	1980	20	3	4,700	8,900		
ETR Star Systems	1951	5	30	6,000	8,000	29,500	70,300
Euclid Computer	1980	1	10	9,300	15,800	24,900	
Exidy Systems Inc.	1978	9	2	4,200			
Facit, Inc.	1967	20	3	3,800			
Findex, Inc.	1977	5	2	7,000	13,400		
Florida Computer Graphics	1981	1	2	13,800	19,800		
Fortune	1981	26	16	6,600	10,500	20,900	38,800
Four-Phase Systems	1969	234	72		35,000	84,000	122,300
Franklin	1981	3	2	4,000			
General Automation	1967	116	16		34,600	54,400	104,300
GIMIX, Inc.	1975	3	24	5,500	11,700	17,300	43,300
Grid Systems Corp.	1979	2	3	9,000			
Heath Company (Zenith)	1926	2	4	2,800	8,900		
Hewlett-Packard	1947	2,200					
85/87			4	5,100	12,400		
125			2	5,800	12,200		
250			7		26,400	40,500	
3000			110		64,900	76,400	107,600

MANUFACTURER	YEAR ESTABLISHED	ANNUAL DP REVENUE (MILLIONS)	MAXIMUM I/Os	ONE-USER FLOPPY DISK SYSTEM	ONE USER, 5+ MB HARD DISK	4 USERS, 20+ MB 2 PRINTERS	10 USERS, 70+ MB 3 PRINTERS
High Technologies	1982	1	5	3,300			
Honeywell	1886	2,000	9,999				
Level 6			160		34,200	41,500	77,400
IBC (Integrated Bus. Comp.)	1979	5	11	7,100	10,200	21,400	
IBM	1911	30,000					
Personal			2	4,000			
Datamaster			3	8,400	17,800		
Series/1			9,999		26,400	50,600	88,700
System/34			16		20,200	43,700	78,400
System/38			80		66,800	79,400	108,200
ICL Inc.	1968	1	9,999	6,900	10,500	36,400	81,900
IMS International	1980	17	16	5,600	11,400	23,300	46,100
Infotecs, Inc.	1976	4	2	10,000			
Intelligent Systems	1973	20	5	7,900	12,400		
Intertec Data Systems	1973	40	255	4,800	9,800	31,300	58,800
Jonos, Ltd.	1979	1	2	4,800	7,800		
Kaypro (Kay Computer)	1982	1	2	2,600	4,600*		
Lanier Business Products	1977	293	2	9,000			
Lazor Systems, Inc.	1978	1	16	15,100	22,700	34,300	55,800
Lexitron (Raytheon)	1970	21	2	5,000			
Logical Business Machines	1975	25	20	6,900	20,700	29,500	48,800
MAD Computer	1982	1	3	3,800	7,800		
Marinchip Systems	1977	1	256	6,600	14,700	23,800	
Martec International	1974	35	8	3,400	8,000	23,600	
MDS Systems (Mohawk)	1965	370	11	11,100	14,300	36,700	

Table A2–3 (continued)

MANUFACTURER	YEAR ESTAB-LISHED	ANNUAL DP REVENUE (MILLIONS)	MAXIMUM I/Os	ONE-USER FLOPPY DISK SYSTEM	ONE USER, 5+ MB HARD DISK	4 USERS, 20+ MB 2 PRINTERS	10 USERS, 70+ MB 3 PRINTERS
Mercator	1979	10	17		18,000	23,100	54,100
Micro Five Corporation	1977	5	11	8,700	12,700	31,600	
Micro Technology Unlimited	1977	1	2	5,600			
Microdata (McDonnell Doug.)	1971	410	127		30,800	36,500	65,800
Micromation, Inc.	1977	15	8	7,900	13,700	26,700	
Microtech	1976	6	37		15,400	27,600	46,600
Molecular Computer	1981	5	64		11,700	36,100	58,800
Monroe Systems	1912	5	3	5,400	6,400		
Morrow Designs	1977	2	4	3,000	9,800		
Multi-Tech Systems	1970	4	2	5,800			
National Semiconductor	1965	380	16	6,800	12,600	19,900	32,400*
NBI, Inc.	1973	109	270	14,800	21,300	34,200	79,100
NCR Corporation	1884	3,200	9,999				
Tower			16		17,800	36,800	70,100
I–9000 Series			24	13,700	17,600	54,900	106,200
NEC Information Systems	1977	125					
Personal			2	4,700			
Astra			32	9,900	25,000	55,800	99,700
Newsmate Products	1978	1	16	8,000	11,600	24,200	
Nixdorf Computer Corp.	1952	185	30		30,800	66,000	127,500
NNC Electronics	1978	4	5	7,100	12,700		
Norpak Ltd.	1975	2	4	10,500			
North Star Computers	1976	25	6	5,200	7,700	23,300	
Northern Telecom, Inc.	1978	250	3	8,400			
Novell Data Systems	1980	6	29			25,600	55,600
Ohio Scientific	1975	50	10	4,800	10,500	20,300	

MANUFACTURER	YEAR ESTAB-LISHED	ANNUAL DP REVENUE (MILLIONS)	MAXIMUM I/Os	ONE-USER FLOPPY DISK SYSTEM	ONE USER, 5+ MB HARD DISK	4 USERS, 20+ MB 2 PRINTERS	10 USERS, 70+ MB 3 PRINTERS
Olivetti	1955	15	3	3,800			
Omnibyte Corporation	1976	3	4		12,900		
Ontel Corporation	1974	25	2	3,800	6,200		
Onyx Systems	1979	35	11		11,600	36,900	
Osborne Computer	1981	4	2	2,600			
OSM Computer Corp.	1980	3	32		7,400	23,100	60,800
Otrona	1977	1	2	4,800			
Paradyne Corporation	1969	240	32		23,000	39,100	75,800
Perkin-Elmer Corp.	1966	250	32		29,400	48,900	93,800
Personal Micro Computers	1980	2	4	2,800			
Pertec Computer Corp.	1967	150					
2000			7	12,500	22,500	34,600	
3000			19		29,100	38,500	73,800
Philips Information (Micom)	1973	202	2	9,000	21,700	31,300	
Plessey Peripheral	1969	50	6				
Point 4 Data Corp.	1969	12	120		34,700	43,300	83,300
Prime Computer	1971	450	128	10,800	44,500	53,800	70,300
Prodigy Systems	1974	5	2		21,800		
Q1 Corporation	1969	5	16	11,400	16,400		
Qantel (Mohawk)	1968	65	64		14,000	48,200	122,400
Quasar Data Products	1978	2	4	6,300	10,900		
Quay Corporation	1977	2	8	3,800	11,900	22,300	
Radio Shack (Tandy)	1921	600					
TRS-80-III			2	3,700	5,700		
TRS-80-II/16			2	5,900	9,700		
Rair Microcomputer	1974	12	8	5,100	9,200	22,800	

Table A2–3 (continued)

MANUFACTURER	YEAR ESTAB-LISHED	ANNUAL DP REVENUE (MILLIONS)	MAXIMUM I/Os	ONE-USER FLOPPY DISK SYSTEM	ONE USER, 5+ MB HARD DISK	4 USERS, 20+ MB 2 PRINTERS	10 USERS, 70+ MB 3 PRINTERS
Rexon Business Machines	1978	7	21		17,600	26,100	55,400
Ridge Computers	1980	1	6		62,800	96,800	
Sage Computer Technology	1981	1	3	6,000			
Sanyo	1980	10	2	4,500			
SD Systems	1976	6	16	5,100	19,800	21,900	68,000
Seiko (Sci-Com)	1982	1	6	6,200	10,400	17,200	
Sharp Electronics	1962	5	4	4,100			
Smoke Signal Broadcasting	1977	4	16	5,500	9,800	21,200	34,200
SOLVation, Inc.	1980	2	3	9,500	16,000		
Solid State Technology	1969	1	8	7,700	12,500	35,600	
Sony	1980	10	2	4,000			
Sperry Univac	1962	3,100	9,999				
80 Series			40		67,800	79,200	116,800
STC Systems (Storage Tech.)	1969	1,300	113		48,500	107,700	154,800
Sumicom Inc.	1982	1	3	6,700			
Syntrex	1979	10	16	10,200	22,200	50,700	112,000
Systems Group	1978	5	20	7,400	10,400	26,300	40,800
TAB Products	1949	10	6		8,000		
Tandem	1974	310	9,999		117,700**	131,600**	164,500**
Tarbell Electronics	1976	1	16	6,300	9,100	21,100	42,100
Tecmar, Inc.	1974	1	6	5,800	13,700	21,300	
Teleram Communications	1973	6	3	4,400			
Televideo Systems	1975	105	19	4,300	8,800	27,500	46,000
Terak	1975	10	4	6,800			

MANUFACTURER	YEAR ESTAB-LISHED	ANNUAL DP REVENUE (MILLIONS)	MAXIMUM I/Os	ONE-USER FLOPPY DISK SYSTEM	ONE USER, 5+ MB HARD DISK	4 USERS, 20+ MB 2 PRINTERS	10 USERS, 70+ MB 3 PRINTERS
Texas Instruments							
220	1930	750	2	7,200	15,100		
990 Series			16		26,000	40,200	73,900
Three Rivers Computer	1974	7	3		31,200		
Toshiba America	1981	4	2	4,000			
TRW-Fujitsu	1980	5	16	8,800	14,200		
Ultimate Corporation	1978	30	126		24,300	33,500	73,500
Vector Graphic	1976	36	4	5,200	9,500		
Vertical Data Systems	1981	1	2	3,900			
Victor Business Products	1917	10	4	5,700	10,500		
Victory Computer	1981	1	16		16,700	26,300	50,800
Wang Laboratories	1951	1,400	128				
Personal			2	9,700			
2200 Series			16	11,500	20,500	36,000	72,500
VS Series			34		36,400	58,600	91,600
Wicat Systems	1976	7	16		11,300	29,200	59,700
Xerox Corporation	1961	1,350	2	4,000			
Zenith Data Systems	1979	117	2	6,300	10,500		
Zilog	1975	30	27		17,800	34,100	75,000
Average				$ 6,375	$ 17,958	$ 36,989	$ 72,501
*Minimum				$ 2,500	$ 4,600	$ 17,100	$ 32,400
**Maximum				$ 15,400	$ 117,700	$ 131,600	$164,500

Table A2–4
SYSTEMS SUMMARIES: ONE-USER FLOPPY DISK
(Two Ports Used)*

MANUFACTURER: MODEL:	AVERAGE 146 SYSTEMS	APPLE IIe	COMMODORE 8032	DEC DECmate	FORTUNE SYSTEM 1
BASE SYSTEM:					
END-USER PRICE, $					
CPU, DISKS & TAPE	$4,446	$2,000	$2,800	$3,900	$5,800
CRTS, MONITORS	876	500	Incl.	Incl.	Incl.
PRINTERS	1,053	800	800	Incl.	800
TOTAL	$6,375	$3,300	$3,600	$3,900	$6,600
WORD SIZE, BITS	10	8	8	12	16/32
CPU MEMORY, K	70	64	32	64	128
DISK, ON-LINE, MB	1.07	.28	.34	.51	1.6
BACK-UP, MB	.54	.14	.17	.26	.8
PRINTERS, cps, dot mtrx	94	120	80	45	80
PTRS SUPL. BY SAME	62% YES	YES	YES	YES	NO
CRTS SUPL. BY SAME	79% YES	YES	YES	YES	YES
SCREEN SIZE	12/1840	12/1920	12/2000	12/1920	12/1920
MAXIMUM UPGRADE:	(MEDIAN)				
CPU MEMORY, K	232	128	96	64	1000
DISK ON-LINE, MB	24	.84	7.5	10	80
BACK-UP, MB	1.2	.14	2.1	.5	17
NO. OF PORTS	6	2	5	2	16
FEATURES AVAILABLE:					
CP/M, MP/M	67%	CP/M			
Unix or Xenix	6%				Unix
OASIS	8%				
Primary Operating System		DOS 3.3	Commodore	OS/78	
BASIC	89%	BASIC	BASIC	BASIC	BASIC
Word Processing	92%	WP	WP	WP	WP
DBMS	80%	DBMS	DBMS		DBMS
Accounting	91%	Acctg.	Acctg.	Acctg.	Acctg.
Simultaneous File					
Access	27%				
CRT Multitasking	10%				
Spooling	27%			Sp	
RS 232 Peripherals	72%	232 Prph			232 Prph
Unlimited (Shared) System	1%				
Software Included		WP			

Table A2–4 (continued)
SYSTEMS SUMMARIES: ONE-USER FLOPPY DISK
(Two Ports Used)*

MANUFACTURER:	IBM	OSBORNE	RADIO SHACK	VECTOR GRAPHIC	XEROX
MODEL:	Personal	I	TRS–80II	4/20	820
BASE SYSTEM:					
END-USER PRICE, $					
CPU, DISKS & TAPE	$3,000	$1,800	$4,700	$2,500	$3,200
CRTS, MONITORS	400	Incl.	Incl.	2,000	Incl.
PRINTERS	600	800	1,200	700	800
TOTAL	$4,000	$2,600	$5,900	$5,200	$4,000
WORD SIZE, BITS	16	8	8	8/16	8
CPU MEMORY, K	64	64	64	128	64
DISK, ON-LINE, MB	.64	.4	.86	1.2	.16
BACK-UP, MB	.32	.2	.48	.6	.08
PRINTERS, cps, dot mtrx	80	80	140	80	80
PRTS SUPL. BY SAME	YES	NO	YES	YES	YES
CRTS SUPL. BY SAME	YES	YES	YES	YES	YES
SCREEN SIZE	12/2000	5/1248	12/1920	12/1920	12/1920
MAXIMUM UPGRADE:					
CPU MEMORY, K	512	64	512	256	64
DISK ON-LINE, MB	.64	.4	34	33	.48
BACK-UP, MB	.32	.2	1.2	15	.24
NO. OF PORTS	2	2	3	4	2
FEATURES AVAILABLE:					
CP/M, MP/M	CP/M	CP/M		C&MP/M	CP/M
Unix or Xenix					
OASIS				OASIS	
Primary Operating System	PC DOS		TRS–DOS2		
BASIC	BASIC	BASIC	BASIC	BASIC	BASIC
Word Processing	WP	WP	WP	WP	WP
DBMS	DBMS	DBMS	DBMS	DBMS	DBMS
Accounting	Acctg.	Acctg.	Acctg.	Acctg.	Acctg.
Simultaneous File Access					
CRT Multitasking					
Spooling				Sp	
RS 232 Peripherals	232 Prph	232 Prph	232 Prph	232 Prph	232 Prph
Unlimited (Shared) System					
Software Included		Sftwr			

* Selected systems for example purposes.

Table A2–5
SYSTEMS SUMMARIES: ONE USER, 5+ MB HARD DISK
(Two Ports Used)*

MANUFACTURER: MODEL:	AVERAGE 160 SYSTEMS	ALTOS 5–5D	APPLE III	BASIC FOUR S/10	COMMODORE 8032
BASE SYSTEM:					
END-USER PRICE, $					
CPU, DISKS & TAPE	$14,419	$6,000	$4,600	$8,500	$6,800
CRTS, MONITORS	1,251	900	300	Incl.	Incl.
PRINTERS	2,288	1,800	1,800	1,500	1,000
TOTAL	$17,958	$8,700	$6,700	$10,000	$7,800
WORD SIZE, BITS	12	8	8	8	8
CPU MEMORY, K	104	192	256	64	96
DISK, ON-LINE, MB	16	5.0	5.0	11	7.5
BACK-UP, MB	8	1.0	.14	1.2	1.0
TYPE	65% FLPY	FLPY	FLPY	FLPY	FLPY
PRINTERS, cps, dot mtrx	144	150	150	120	150
PRTS SUPL. BY SAME	61% YES	NO	YES	YES	YES
CRTS SUPL. BY SAME	73% YES	NO	YES	YES	YES
SCREEN SIZE	12/1940	12/1920	12/1920	12/1920	12/2000
MAXIMUM UPGRADE:	(MEDIAN)				
CPU MEMORY, K	512	208	256	8000	96
DISK ON-LINE, MB	88	40	5.0	2400	7.5
BACK-UP, MB	20	17	.14	80	2.1
NO. OF PORTS	16	7	2	64	2
FEATURES AVAILABLE:					
CP/M, MP/M	41%	C&MP/M	CP/M	CP/M	
Unix or Xenix	9%				
OASIS	9%	OASIS			
Primary Operating System			SOS	BOSS	Commodore
BASIC	93%	BASIC	BASIC	BASIC	BASIC
Word Processing	86%	WP	WP	WP	WP
DBMS	75%	DBMS	DBMS	DBMS	DBMS
Accounting	90%	Acctg.	Acctg.	Acctg.	Acctg.
Simultaneous File Access	58%	SFA			
CRT Multitasking	33%				
Spooling	54%	Sp			
RS 232 Peripherals	75%	232 Prph	232 Prph	232 Prph	
Unlimited (Shared) System	4%				
Software Included			WP		

Table A2–5 (continued)
SYSTEMS SUMMARIES: ONE USER, 5+ MB HARD DISK
(Two Ports Used)*

MANUFACTURER:	FORTUNE	IBM	NORTH STAR	RADIO SHACK	VECTOR GRAPHIC
MODEL:	System 2	System/34	Horizon	TRS–80–16	4/30
BASE SYSTEM:					
END-USER PRICE, $					
CPU, DISKS & TAPE	$ 8,700	$14,100	$5,000	$8,500	$4,000
CRTS, MONITORS	Incl.	2,100	900	Incl.	2,000
PRINTERS	1,800	4,000	1,800	1,200	3,500
TOTAL	$10,500	$20,200	$7,700	$9,700	$9,500
WORD SIZE, BITS	16/32	16	8	16	8/16
CPU MEMORY, K	128	64	64	128	128
DISK, ON-LINE, MB	5.0	9.6	5.0	8.4	5.6
BACK-UP, MB	.8	1.2	.4	1.2	.6
TYPE	FLPY	FLPY	FLPY	FLPY	FLPY
PRINTERS, cps, dot mtrx	150	140	150	140	
cps, letter					35
PTRS SUPL. BY SAME	NO	YES	NO	YES	YES
CRTS SUPL. BY SAME	YES	YES	NO	YES	YES
SCREEN SIZE	12/1920	12/1920	12/1920	12/1920	12/1920
MAXIMUM UPGRADE:					
CPU MEMORY, K	1000	256	344	512	256
DISK ON-LINE, MB	80	257	72	34	33
BACK-UP, MB	17	27	13	1.2	15
NO. OF PORTS	16	16	6	3	4
FEATURES AVAILABLE:					
CP/M, MP/M			CP/M		C&MP/M
Unix or Xenix	Unix				
OASIS					OASIS
Primary Operating System		IBM/34	TSS/A&C	TRS–DOS2	
BASIC	BASIC		BASIC	BASIC	BASIC
Word Processing	WP		WP	WP	WP
DBMS	DBMS		DBMS	DBMS	DBMS
Accounting	Acctg.	Acctg.	Acctg.	Acctg.	Acctg.
Simultaneous File Access		SFA			
CRT Multitasking		Mlt			
Spooling		Sp			Sp
RS 232 Peripherals	232 Prph		232 Prph	232 Prph	232 Prph
Unlimited (Shared) System					
Software Included					

* Selected systems for example purposes.

Table A2–6
SYSTEMS SUMMARIES: FOUR USERS, TWO PRINTERS
(Six Ports Used), 20+ MB*

MANUFACTURER:	AVERAGE 112	ALPHA MICRO	ALTOS	BASIC FOUR	BURROUGHS
MODEL:	SYSTEMS	AM–1042	8600–14	S/80	B 92
BASE SYSTEM:					
END-USER PRICE, $					
CPU, DISKS & TAPE	$24,859	$20,800	$17,000	$27,000	$25,000
CRTS, MONITORS	6,358	4,000	4,000	7,000	11,600
PRINTERS	5,772	4,300	4,300	5,000	5,700
TOTAL	$36,989	$29,100	$25,300	$39,000	$42,300
WORD SIZE, BITS	12	16/32	16	8	8
CPU MEMORY, K	215	128	512	320	608
DISK, ON-LINE, MB	29	32	40	20	38
BACK-UP, MB	16	100	17	20	20
TYPE	36% FLPY	VCR	TAPE	TAPE	TAPE
PRINTERS, cps, dot mtrx	147	150	150	120	120
cps, letter	52	40	40	50	45
PTRS SUPL. BY SAME	59% YES	NO	NO	YES	YES
CRTS SUPL. BY SAME	71% YES	NO	NO	YES	YES
SCREEN SIZE	12/1980	12/1920	12/1920	12/1920	12/2000
MAXIMUM UPGRADE:	(MEDIAN)				
CPU MEMORY, K	1000	4096	1000	8000	512
DISK ON-LINE, MB	100	2400	80	2400	77
BACK-UP, MB	24	100	100	80	20
NO. OF PORTS	18	68	17	64	8
FEATURES AVAILABLE:					
CP/M, MP/M	40%		C&MP/M	CP/M	
Unix or Xenix	12%		Xenix		
OASIS	9%		OASIS		
Primary Operating System		AMOS		BOSS	MCP II
BASIC	88%	BASIC	BASIC	BASIC	
Word Processing	87%	WP	WP	WP	
DBMS	76%	DBMS	DBMS	DBMS	
Accounting	94%	Acctg.	Acctg.	Acctg.	Acctg.
Simultaneous File Access	83%	SFA	SFA	SFA	SFA
CRT Multitasking	48%				
Spooling	73%	Sp	Sp	Sp	Sp
RS 232 Peripherals	67%	232 Prph	232 Prph	232 Prph	
Unlimited (Shared) System Software Included	5%				

Table A2–6 (continued)
SYSTEMS SUMMARIES: FOUR USERS, TWO PRINTERS
(Six Ports Used), 20+ MB*

MANUFACTURER: MODEL:	DATA GENERAL Nova 4X	DEC PDP 11/23+	EAGLE 1600	FORTUNE System 10	IBM System/34
BASE SYSTEM:					
END-USER PRICE, $					
CPU, DISKS & TAPE	$21,000	$20,800	$10,000	$12,200	$27,100
CRTS, MONITORS	7,000	7,800	9,000	4,400	8,400
PRINTERS	9,600	6,100	4,300	4,300	8,200
TOTAL	$37,600	$34,700	$23,300	$20,900	$43,700
WORD SIZE, BITS	16	16	16	16/32	16
CPU MEMORY, K	128	256	320	256	96
DISK, ON-LINE, MB	20	21	40	20	27
BACK-UP, MB	10	10	.8	17	27
TYPE	DISK	DISK	FLPY	TAPE	FLPY
PRINTERS, cps, dot mtrx	180	180	150	150	140
cps, letter	60	45	40	40	40
PTRS SUPL. BY SAME	YES	YES	NO	NO	YES
CRTS SUPL. BY SAME	YES	YES	YES	YES	YES
SCREEN SIZE	12/1920	14/3168	12/1920	12/1920	12/1920
MAXIMUM UPGRADE:					
CPU MEMORY, K	2048	4000	640	1000	256
DISK ON-LINE, MB	6600	2048	40	80	257
BACK-UP, MB	80	40	1.0	17	27
NO. OF PORTS	64	127	11	16	16
FEATURES AVAILABLE:					
CP/M, MP/M			C&MP/M		
Unix or Xenix				Unix	
OASIS					
Primary Operating System	RDOS	RTS/E	MS–DOS		IBM/34
BASIC	BASIC		BASIC	BASIC	
Word Processing	WP	WP	WP	WP	
DBMS		DBMS	DBMS	DBMS	
Accounting	Acctg.	Acctg.	Acctg.	Acctg.	Acctg.
Simultaneous File Access	SFA	SFA			SFA
CRT Multitasking	Mlt	Mlt			Mlt
Spooling	Sp	Sp			Sp
RS 232 Peripherals	232 Prph	232 Prph	232 Prph	232 Prph	
Unlimited (Shared) System					
Software Included			Sftwr		

Table A2–6 (continued)
SYSTEMS SUMMARIES: FOUR USERS, TWO PRINTERS
(Six Ports Used), 20+ MB*

MANUFACTURER:	MICRODATA	NCR	POINT 4	TEXAS INSTRUMENTS	WANG
MODEL:	4700	I–9020	Mark V	S672	2200LVP
BASE SYSTEM:					
END-USER PRICE, $					
CPU, DISKS & TAPE	$27,000	$38,100	$35,000	$31,000	$24,000
CRTS, MONITORS	4,000	8,000	4,000	4,400	4,000
PRINTERS	5,500	8,800	4,300	4,800	8,000
TOTAL	$36,500	$54,900	$43,300	$40,200	$36,000
WORD SIZE, BITS	16	16	16	16	8/24
CPU MEMORY, K	64	256	64	256	128
DISK, ON-LINE, MB	32	54	28	43	20
BACK-UP, MB	40	27	14	19	10
TYPE	TAPE	DISK	DISK	TAPE	DISK
PRINTERS, cps, dot mtrx	180	2/240	150	2/150	180
cps, letter	35	NA	40	NA	30
PTRS SUPL. BY SAME	YES	YES	NO	YES	YES
CRTS SUPL. BY SAME	YES	YES	NO	YES	YES
SCREEN SIZE	12/1920	12/1920	12/1920	12/1920	12/1920
MAXIMUM UPGRADE:					
CPU MEMORY, K	2000	3072	512	2000	512
DISK ON-LINE, MB	1000	14160	320	320	480
BACK-UP, MB	60	27	40	40	50
NO. OF PORTS	127	24	120	16	16
FEATURES AVAILABLE:					
CP/M, MP/M					
Unix or Xenix					
OASIS					
Primary Operating System	Reality	IRX	IRIS	DX1O	2200
BASIC	BASIC	BASIC	BASIC	BASIC	BASIC
Word Processing	WP		WP	WP	WP
DBMS	DBMS		DBMS	DBMS	
Accounting	Acctg.	Acctg.	Acctg.	Acctg.	Acctg.
Simultaneous File					
Access	SFA	SFA	SFA	SFA	SFA
CRT Multitasking	Mlt	Mlt	Mlt	Mlt	Mlt
Spooling	Sp	Sp	Sp	Sp	Sp
RS 232 Peripherals	232 Prph		232 Prph	232 Prph	
Unlimited (Shared) System					
Software Included					

* Selected systems for example purposes.

Table A2–7
SYSTEMS SUMMARIES: TEN USERS, THREE PRINTERS
(Thirteen Ports Used), 70+ MB*

MANUFACTURER:	AVERAGE 77	ALPHA MICRO	BASIC FOUR	BURROUGHS	DATA GENERAL
MODEL:	SYSTEMS	AM–1062	510	B 920	Eclipse
BASE SYSTEM:					
END-USER PRICE, $					
CPU, DISKS & TAPE	$47,099	$27,000	$85,000	$44,800	$58,300
CRTS, MONITORS	11,031	10,000	24,000	29,000	17,500
PRINTERS	14,371	10,800	14,500	17,200	17,100
TOTAL	$72,501	$47,800	$123,500	$91,000	$92,900
WORD SIZE, BITS	14	16/32	16	8	16
CPU MEMORY, K	438	512	160	608	384
DISK, ON-LINE, MB	81	60	70	77	96
BACK-UP, MB	34	100	35	20	48
TYPE	48% TAPE	VCR	DISK	TAPE	DISK
PRINTERS, cps, dot mtrx	147	150	120	120	180
cps, letter	61	40	50	45	60
lpm	299	300	300	320	300
PTRS SUPL. BY SAME	67% YES	NO	YES	YES	YES
CRTS SUPL. BY SAME	78% YES	NO	YES	YES	YES
SCREEN SIZE	12/1950	12/1920	12/1920	12/2000	12/1920
MAXIMUM UPGRADE:	(MEDIAN)				
CPU MEMORY, K	1012	4096	8000	1536	2048
DISK ON-LINE, MB	300	2400	2400	390	6600
BACK-UP, MB	40	100	80	50	80
NO. OF PORTS	32	68	64	36	64
FEATURES AVAILABLE:					
CP/M, MP/M	38%		CP/M		
Unix or Xenix	12%				
OASIS	7%				
Primary Operating System		AMOS	BOSS	MCP	RDOS
BASIC	90%	BASIC	BASIC		BASIC
Word Processing	91%	WP	WP		WP
DBMS	82%	DBMS	DBMS		
Accounting	97%	Acctg.	Acctg.	Acctg.	Acctg.
Simultaneous File Access	95%	SFA	SFA	SFA	SFA
CRT Multitasking	58%	Mlt			Mlt
Spooling	83%	Sp	Sp	Sp	Sp
RS 232 Peripherals	68%	232 Prph	232 Prph		232 Prph
Unlimited (Shared) System Software Included	8%				

Table A2–7 (continued)
SYSTEMS SUMMARIES: TEN USERS, THREE PRINTERS
(Thirteen Ports Used), 70+ MB*

MANUFACTURER:	DEC PDP	FORTUNE	IBM	MICRO DATA	NCR
MODEL:	11/44	System 10	System/38	4700	I–9040
BASE SYSTEM:					
END-USER PRICE, $					
CPU, DISKS & TAPE	$ 72,000	$17,000	$ 60,000	$42,600	$ 65,100
CRTS, MONITORS	19,500	11,000	28,000	11,000	20,000
PRINTERS	21,400	10,800	20,200	12,200	21,100
TOTAL	$112,900	$38,800	$108,200	$65,800	$106,200
WORD SIZE, BITS	16	16/32	16	16	32
CPU MEMORY, K	512	512	512	128	512
DISK, ON-LINE, MB	122	80	65	80	81
BACK-UP, MB	40	17	24	40	14
TYPE	TAPE	TAPE	FLPY	TAPE	DISK
PRINTERS, cps, dot mtrx	180	150	140	180	2/240
cps, letter	45	40	40	35	NA
lpm	600	300	300	300	200
PTRS SUPL. BY SAME	YES	NO	YES	YES	YES
CRTS SUPL. BY SAME	YES	YES	YES	YES	YES
SCREEN SIZE	14/3168	12/1920	12/1920	12/1920	12/1920
MAXIMUM UPGRADE:					
CPU MEMORY, K	4000	1000	2048	2000	3072
DISK ON-LINE, MB	2048	80	2286	1000	14160
BACK-UP, MB	40	17	50	60	27
NO. OF PORTS	127	16	80	127	24
FEATURES AVAILABLE:					
CP/M, MP/M					
Unix or Xenix		Unix			
OASIS					
Primary Operating System	RTS/E		IBM/38	Reality	IRX
BASIC		BASIC		BASIC	BASIC
Word Processing	WP	WP		WP	
DBMS	DBMS	DBMS	DBMS	DBMS	
Accounting	Acctg.	Acctg.	Acctg.	Acctg.	Acctg.
Simultaneous File					
Access	SFA		SFA	SFA	SFA
CRT Multitasking	Mlt		Mlt	Mlt	Mlt
Spooling	Sp		Sp	Sp	Sp
RS 232 Peripherals	232 Prph	232 Prph		232 Prph	
Unlimited (Shared) System					
Software Included					

Table A2–7 (continued)
SYSTEMS SUMMARIES: TEN USERS, THREE PRINTERS
(Thirteen Ports Used), 70 + MB*

MANUFACTURER:	PRIME	TANDEM	TELEVIDEO	TEXAS INSTRUMENTS	WANG
MODEL:	2250	NonStop	TS 816	S682	2200MVP
BASE SYSTEM:					
END-USER PRICE, $					
CPU, DISKS & TAPE	$39,900	$110,000	$15,200	$49,500	$35,500
CRTS, MONITORS	14,400	31,500	20,000	11,000	20,000
PRINTERS	16,000	23,000	10,800	13,400	17,000
TOTAL	$70,300	$164,500	$46,000	$73,900	$72,500
WORD SIZE, BITS	32	16	8	16	8/24
CPU MEMORY, K	512	384	768	512	256
DISK, ON-LINE, MB	68	64	40	80	67
BACK-UP, MB	15	50	20	40	13
TYPE	TAPE	TAPE	TAPE	TAPE	DISK
PRINTERS, cps, dot mtrx	200	2/200	150	2/150	180
cps, letter	55	NA	40	NA	30
lpm	300	600	300	300	300
PTRS SUPL. BY SAME	YES	YES	YES	YES	YES
CRTS SUPL. BY SAME	YES	YES	YES	YES	YES
SCREEN SIZE	12/1920	2/2000	12/1920	12/1920	12/1920
MAXIMUM UPGRADE:					
CPU MEMORY, K	8000	2000	1000	2000	512
DISK ON-LINE, MB	5040	Unlimited	40	320	480
BACK-UP, MB	68	240	20	40	50
NO. OF PORTS	128	Unlimited	19	16	16
FEATURES AVAILABLE:					
CP/M, MP/M			CP/M		
Unix or Xenix					
OASIS					
Primary Operating System	PRIMOS	Guardian	MmmOST	DX10	2200
BASIC	BASIC		BASIC	BASIC	BASIC
Word Processing	WP		WP	WP	WP
DBMS	DBMS		DBMS	DBMS	
Accounting	Acctg.	Acctg.	Acctg.	Acctg.	Acctg.
Simultaneous File Access	SFA	SFA	SFA	SFA	SFA
CRT Multitasking	Mlt	Mlt		Mlt	Mlt
Spooling	Sp	Sp	Sp	Sp	Sp
RS 232 Peripherals	232 Prph		232 Prph	232 Prph	
Unlimited (Shared) System Software Included		Unlimited			

* Selected systems for example purposes.

DIRECTORY OF
COMPUTER MANUFACTURERS

Access Matrix Corporation, 2159 Bering Drive, San Jose, CA 95131 (408) 263–3660

Action Computer Enterprise, Inc., 55 West Del Mar Boulevard, Pasadena, CA 91105 (213) 793–2440

ADDS (Applied Digital Data Systems, Inc.), 100 Marcus Boulevard, Hauppauge, NY 11787 (516) 231–5400

Alpha Microsystems, 17881 Sky Park North, P. O. Box 18347, Irvine, CA 92713 (714) 641-0386

Alspa Computers, Inc., 300 Harvey West Boulevard, Santa Cruz, CA 95060 (408) 429–6000

Altos Computer Systems, 2360 Bering Drive, San Jose, CA 95131 (408) 946–6700

Apple Computer, Inc., 20525 Mariani Avenue, Cupertino, CA 95014 (408) 996–1010

Archives, Inc., 404 West 35th Street, Davenport, IA 52806 (800) 553–6950

Ardent Computer Products, Inc., 145 Palisades Street, Dobbs Ferry, NY 10522 (914) 693–6900

Atari, Inc., Home Computer Division, a Warner Communications Company, 1312 Crossman, Sunnyvale, CA 94086 (408) 942–6500

ATV Jacquard, Inc., 2921 S. Daimler Road, Santa Ana, CA 92711 (714) 546–3551

Barrington International, 738 Airport Boulevard, Suite 4, Ann Arbor, MI 48104 (313) 769–7611

Basic Four Information Systems Division, Management Assistance, Inc., 14101 Myford Road, Tustin, CA 92680 (714) 731–5100

Beehive International, 4910 Amelia Earhart Drive, Box 25688, Salt Lake City, UT 84125 (800) 453–9454

Billings Computer Corporation, 18600 E. 37th Terrace South, Independence, MO 64057 (816) 373–0000

Blackhawk Computer System, 426 West 2nd Street, Davenport, IA 52081 (319) 323–7857

BMC Computer Corporation, 860 E. Walnut Street, Carson, CA 90746 (213) 323–2600

BTI Computer Systems, 870 W. Maude Avenue, Sunnyvale, CA 94086 (408) 733–1122

Burr-Brown Research Corporation, Industrial Systems Products Division, 3631 East 44th Street, Tuscon, AZ 85713 (602) 747–0711

Burroughs Corporation, Burroughs Place, Detroit, MI 48232 (313) 972–7000

Bytronix Corporation, 2701 E. Chapman Avenue, Fullerton, CA 92631 (714) 871–8763

Cado Systems Corporation, 2771 Toledo Street, Torrance, CA 90503 (213) 320–9660

Canon, U.S.A., Inc., One Canon Plaza, Lake Success, NY 11042 (516) 488–6700

CAPRO Incorporated, 12781 Pala Drive, Garden Grove, CA 92641 (714) 891-1109

Casio, Inc., Microcomputer Division, 15 Gardner Road, Fairfield, NJ 07006 (201) 575–7400

Centurion Computer Corporation, 1780 Jay Ell Drive, Richardson, TX 75081 (214) 699–8400

Century Computer Corporation, 14453 Gillis Road, Dallas, TX 95234 (214) 233–3238

Challenge Systems, Inc., 1299 Commerce Drive, Richardson, TX 95081 (214) 669–1101

Chromatics, Inc., 2558 Mountain Industrial Boulevard, Tucker, GA 30084 (404) 493–7000

CIE Systems, 2515 McCabe Way, P. O. Box 16579, Irvine, CA 92713 (714) 957–1112

Codata Systems Corporation, 285 N. Wolfe Road, Sunnyvale, CA 94086 (408) 735–1744

CODEX (Motorola, Inc.), 20 Cabot Boulevard, Mansfield, MA 02048 (617) 364–2000

Colonial Data Sciences Corporation, 105 Sanford Street, Hamden, CT 06514 (203) 288–2524

Columbia Data Products, 8990 Route 108, Columbia, MD 21045 (301) 992–3400

Commodore Business Machines, Inc., Computer Systems Division, 487 Devon Park Drive, Wayne, PA 19087 (215) 681–9750

Compal, Inc., 6300 Variel Avenue, Woodland Hills, CA 91367 (213) 992–4425

Comptek Research, Inc., One Technology Center, 45 Oak Street, Buffalo, NY 14203 (716) 842–2700

Compucorp, 1901 South Bundy Drive, Los Angeles, CA 90025 (213) 820–2503

CompuPro Systems, Bldg. 725, Oakland Airport, CA 94614 (415) 562–0636

Computer Automation, 2181 Dupont Drive, Irvine, CA 92713 (714) 833–8830

Computer Devices, Inc., 24 North Avenue, Burlington, MA 01803 (617) 273–1550

Computer Talk, P. O. Box 148, Idledale, CO 80465 (303) 697–5485

Convergent Technologies, Inc., 2500 Augustine Drive, Santa Clara, CA 95051 (408) 727–8830

Corvus Systems, Inc., 2029 O'Toole, San Jose, CA 95131 (408) 946–7700

CPT Corporation, 8100 Mitchell Road, P. O. Box 295, Minneapolis, MN 55440 (612) 937–8000

Cromemco, Inc., 280 Bernardo Avenue, Mountain View, CA 94040 (415) 964–7400

Cybersystems, Inc., 8300 Whitesburg Drive, Huntsville, AL 35802 (205) 883–4410

Data General Corporation, 4400 Computer Drive, Westboro, MA 01580 (617) 366–8911

Data Systems Marketing, 5710 Ruffin Road, San Diego, CA 92123 (619) 560–9222

Data Technology Industries (formerly Gnat Computers), 701-A Whitney Street, San Leandro, CA 94577 (415) 638–1206

Datamac Computer Systems, Inc., 680 Almanor Avenue, Sunnyvale, CA 94086 (408) 735–0323

Datapoint Corporation, 9725 Datapoint Drive, San Antonio, TX 78284 (512) 699–7000

Datavue Corporation, 1911 22nd Avenue South, Seattle, WA 98144 (206) 322–9330, (800) 426–9247

DEC (Digital Equipment Corporation), 146 Main Street, Maynard, MA 01754 (617) 897–5111

Delta Data Systems Corporation, 2595 Metropolitan Drive, Trevrose, PA 19047 (215) 639–9400

Digital Computer Corporation, 7430 Trade Street, San Diego, CA 92121 (619) 566–8500

Digital Microsystems, Inc., 1840 Embarcadero, Oakland, CA 94606 (415) 532–3686

Digital Systems Corporation, 114 East Gregory Street, Pensacola, FL 32501 (904) 434–2685

Distributed Computer Systems, 223 Crescent Street, Waltham, MA 02154 (617) 899–6619

Durango Systems, Inc., 3003 N. First Street, San Jose, CA 95134 (408) 946–5000

Dynabyte, Inc., 521 Cottonwood Drive, Milpitas, CA 95035 (408) 263–1221

E & H Electronics, 2699 East 28th Street, Suite 416, Signal Hill, CA 90806 (213) 426–3327

Eagle Computer Inc., 983 University Avenue, Los Gatos, CA 95030 (408) 395–5005

Epic Computer Corporation, 7542 Trade Street, San Diego, CA 92121 (714) 695–3560

ETR Star Systems, 1316 North Avalon Boulevard, Wilmington, CA 90744 (213) 835–2421

Euclid Computer, 3699 West 240th Street, Torrance, CA 90505 (213) 373–9316

Exidy Systems, Inc., 1234 Elko Drive, Sunnyvale, CA 94086 (408) 734–9831

Facit, Inc., 235 Main Dunstable Road, Nashua, NH 03061 (603) 883–4157

Findex, Inc., 20775 South Western Avenue, Torrance, CA 90501 (213) 533–6842

Florida Computer Graphics, 100 Sand Pond Road, Lake Mary, FL 32746 (305) 321–3000

Fortune Systems, 1501 Industrial Road, San Carlos, CA 94070 (415) 595–8444

Four–Phase Systems, Inc., 10700 North De Anza Boulevard, Cupertino, CA 95014 (408) 255–0900

Franklin Computer Corporation, 7030 Colonial Highway, Pennsauken, NJ 08109 (609) 488–1700

General Automation, Inc., 1055 S. East Street, P. O. Box 4883, Anaheim, CA 92805 (714) 778–4800

GIMIX, Inc., 1337 West 37 Place, Chicago, IL 60609 (312) 927–5510

Grid Systems Corporation, 2535 Garcia Avenue, Mountain View, CA 94043 (415) 961–4800

Heath Company (Zenith Radio), Benton Harbor, MI 49022 (616) 982–3200

Hewlett-Packard Company, Personal Computer Division, 1010 NE Circle Boulevard, Corvalis, OR 97330 (503) 757–2000

Hewlett-Packard Company, 19447 Pruneridge Avenue, Cupertino, CA 94014 (408) 725–8111

Hewlett-Packard Company, 1501 Page Mill Road, Palo Alto, CA 94304 (408) 725–8111

High Technologies, Inc., P. O. Box 953, Sandy, UT 84091 (801) 264–8303

Honeywell Information Systems, Inc., 200 Smith Street, Waltham, MA 02154 (617) 895–6000

IBC (Integrated Business Computers), 21592 Marilla Street, Chatsworth, CA 91311 (213) 882–9007

IBM Corporation, General Systems Division, 4111 Northside Parkway NW, P. O. Box 2150, Atlanta, GA 30342 (404) 238–2000

IBM Corporation, National Marketing Division, 4111 Northside Parkway NW, P. O. Box 2150, Atlanta, GA 30327 (404) 238–2000

IBM Corporation, (Personal Computer) Systems Products Division, P. O. Box 1328, Boca Raton, FL 33432 (305) 998–6007

IBM Corporation, Information Systems Group, 1133 Westchester Avenue, White Plains, NY 10604 (914) 696–1900

ICL Inc., 415 East Airport Freeway, Irving, TX 75062 (214) 258–8525

IMS International (formerly Industrial Micro Systems), 2800 Lockheed Way, Carson City, NV 89701 (702) 883–7611

Infotecs, Inc., One Perimeter Road, Manchester, NH 03103 (603) 624–2700

Intelligent Systems Corporation, 225 Technology Park, Norcross, GA 30092 (404) 449–5961

Intertec Data Systems Corporation, 2300 Broad River Road, Columbia, SC 29210 (803) 798–9100

Jonos, Ltd., 920-C East Orangethorpe, Anaheim, CA 92801 (714) 871–1082

Kaypro (Kay Computer), 533 Stevens Avenue, Solona Beach, CA 92075 (619) 755–1134

Lanier Business Products, Inc., 1700 Chantilly Drive NE, Atlanta, GA 30324 (404) 329–8000

Lazor Systems, Inc., 1050 East Duane Avenue, Suite B, Sunnyvale, CA 94086 (408) 735–1188

Lexitron Corporation (Raytheon), 1840 DeHaviland Drive, Thousand Oaks, CA 91359 (805) 499–5911

Logical Machine Corporation, 1294 Hammerwood Avenue, Sunnyvale, CA 94086 (408) 744–1290

MAD Computer, 3350 Scott Boulevard, Bldg. 13, Santa Clara, CA 95051 (408) 980–0840

Marinchip Systems, 16 St. Jude Road, Mill Valley, CA 94941 (415) 383–1545

Martec International Electronics Corporation, 20 William Street, Wellesley, MA 02181 (617) 237–2115

MDS Systems (Mohawk), 7 Century Drive, Parsippany, NJ 07054 (201) 540–9080

Mercator Business Systems, 1294 Lawrence Station Road, Sunnyvale, CA 94086 (408) 734–5134

Micro Five Corporation, 17791 Sky Park Circle, Irvine, CA 92714 (714) 957–1517

Micro Technology Unlimited, 2806 Hillsborough Street, Raleigh, NC 27605 (919) 833–1458

Microdata Corporation, 17481 Red Hill Avenue, Irvine, CA 92714 (714) 540–6730

Micromation, Inc., 1620 Montgomery Street, San Francisco, CA 94111 (415) 398–0289

Microtech Business Systems, 3180 Pullman Street, Costa Mesa, CA 92626 (714) 557–8640

Molecular Computer, 1841 Zanker Road, San Jose, CA 95112 (408) 995–5440

Monroe Systems for Business, The American Road, Morris Plains, NJ 07950 (201) 540–7300

Morrow Designs, Inc., 600 McCormack Street, San Leandro, CA 94577 (415) 430–1970

Multi-Tech Systems, Inc., 82 Second Avenue, SE, New Brighton, MN 55112 (612) 631–3550

National Semiconductor Corporation, 2900 Semiconductor Drive, Santa Clara, CA 95051 (408) 737–5000

NBI, Inc., 1695 38th Street, P. O. Box 9001, Boulder, CO 80301 (303) 444–5710

NCR Corporation, 1700 South Patterson Boulevard, Dayton, OH 45479 (513) 449–2000

NEC Information Systems, Inc., 5 Militia Drive, Lexington, MA 02173 (617) 862–3120

Newsmate Products, Inc., 23 E. Main, Mooresville, IN 46158 (317) 831–0159

Nixdorf Computer Corporation, 168 Middlesex Turnpike, Burlington, MA 01803 (617) 273–0480

NNC Electronics, 15631 Computer Lane, Huntington Beach, CA 92649 (714) 895–8000

Norpak Ltd., 10 Hearst Way, Kanata, Ontario K2L 2P4 (613) 592–4164

North Star Computers, Inc., 14440 Catalina Street, San Leandro, CA 94577 (415) 357–8500

Northern Telecom, Inc., P. O. Box 1222, Minneapolis, MN 55440 (612) 932–8000

Novell Data Systems, Inc., 1170 North Industrial Park Drive, Orem, UT 84057 (801) 226–8202

Ohio Scientific, 7 Oak Park, Bedford, MA 01730 (617) 275–4440

Olivetti Corporation, 155 White Plains Road, Tarrytown, NY 10591 (914) 631–8100

Omnibyte Corporation, 245 W. Roosevelt Road, West Chicago, IL 60185 (312) 231–6880

Ontel Corporation, 250 Crossways Park Drive, Woodbury, NY 11797 (516) 364–2121

Onyx Systems, Inc., 25 E. Trimble Road, San Jose, CA 95131 (408) 946–6330

Osborne Computer Corporation, 26500 Corporate Avenue, Hayward, CA 94545 (415) 887–8080

OSM Computer Corporation, 2364 Walsh Avenue, Santa Clara, CA 95051 (408) 496–6910

Otrona Corporation, 4755 Walnut Street, Boulder, CO 80301 (303) 444–8100

Paradyne Corporation, 8550 Ulmerton Road, P. O. Box 2826, Largo, FL 33540 (815) 530–2000

Perkin-Elmer Corporation, Data Systems Group, 2 Crescent Place, Oceanport, NJ 07757 (201) 870–4500

Personal Micro Computers, Inc., 475 Ellis Street, Mountain View, CA 94043 (415) 962–0220

Pertec Computer Corporation, Data Systems Division, 17112 Armstrong Avenue, Irvine, CA 92714 (714) 540–8340

Philips Information Systems, Inc. (Micom), 4040 McEwen, Dallas, TX 75234 (214) 386–5580

Plessey Peripheral Systems, 17466 Daimler, Irvine, CA 92714 (714) 540–9945

Point 4 Data Corporation, 2569 McCabe Way, Irvine, CA 92714 (714) 754–4114

Prime Computer, Inc., Prime Park, Natick, MA 01760 (617) 655–8000

Prodigy Systems, Inc., 497 Lincoln Highway, Iselin, NJ 08830 (201) 283–2000

Q1 Corporation, 125 Ricefield Lane, Hauppauge, NY 11788 (516) 543–7800

Qantel Corporation, 4142 Point Eden Way, Hayward, CA 94545 (415) 887–7777

Quasar Data Products, Inc., 10330 Brecksville Road, Cleveland, OH 44141 (216) 526–0838

Quay Corporation, 527 Industrial Way West, P. O. Box 783, Eatontown, NJ 07724 (201) 542–7340

Radio Shack (Tandy), 1300 One Tandy Center, Fort Worth, TX 76102 (817) 390–3272

Rair Microcomputer Corporation, 4101 Burton Drive, Santa Clara, CA 95050 (408) 988–1790

Rexon Business Machines Corporation, 5800 Uplander Way, Culver City, CA 90230 (213) 641–7110

Ridge Computers, 586 Weddell Drive, Sunnyvale, CA 94086 (408) 745–0400

Sage Computer Technology, 35 North Edison Way, Suite 4, Reno, NV 89502 (702) 322–6868

Sanyo Business Systems Corporation, 51 Joseph Street, Moonachie, NJ 07074 (201) 440–9300

SD Systems, P. O. Box 28810, Dallas TX 75228 (214) 271–4667

Seiko (Sci-Com Computer Systems), 981 Route 22, P. O. Box 6050, Bridgewater, NJ 08807 (201) 685–0070

Sharp Electronics Corporation, 10 Keystone Place, Paramus, NJ 07652 (201) 265–5600

Smoke Signal Broadcasting, 31336 Via Colinas, Westlake Village, CA 91362 (213) 889–9340

Solid State Technology, Inc., 160 New Boston Street, Woburn, MA 01801 (617) 935–3910

SOLVation, Inc., 400-1 Totten Pond Road, Waltham, MA 02154 (617) 890–8830

Sony Microcomputer Products Division, 7 Mercedes Drive, Montvale, NJ 07645 (201) 573–8899

Sperry Univac, P. O. Box 500, Blue Bell, PA 19424 (215) 542–4011

STC Systems, Inc., Four North Street, Waldwick, NJ 07463 (201) 445–5050

Sumicom, Inc. 17862 E. 17th Street, Tustin, CA 92680 (714) 730–6061

Syntrex Incorporated, 246 Industrial Way West, Eatontown, NJ 07724 (201) 542–1500

Systems Group, 1601 Orangewood, Orange, CA 92668 (714) 633–4460

TAB Products Company, Electronic Office Products Division, 1451 California Avenue, Palo Alto, CA 94304 (415) 858–2500

Tandem Computers, Inc., 19333 Vallco Parkway, Cupertino, CA 95014 (408) 725–6000

Tarbell Electronics, 950 Dovlen Place, Carson, CA 90746 (213) 538–4251

Tecmar, Inc., 23600 Mercantile Road, Cleveland, OH 44122 (216) 464–7410

Teleram Communications Corporation, 2 Corporate Park Drive, White Plains, NY 10604 (914) 694–9270

TeleVideo Systems, Inc., 1170 Morse Avenue, Sunnyvale, CA 94086 (408) 745–7760

Terak Corporation, 14151 North 76th Street, Scottsdale, AZ 85260 (602) 998–4800

Texas Instruments, Inc., P. O. Box 225474, Dallas, TX 75265 (214) 995–2011

Three Rivers Computer Corporation, 720 Gross Street, Pittsburgh, PA 15234 (412) 621–6250

Toshiba America, Inc., Information Processing Systems Division, 2441 Michelle Drive, Tustin, CA 92680 (714) 730–5000

TRW-Fujitsu Company, 9841 Airport Boulevard, Suite 600, Los Angeles, CA 90045 (213) 642–4706

Ultimate Corporation, 77 Brant Avenue, Clark, NJ 07066 (201) 388–8800

Vector Graphics, Inc., 500 N. Ventu Park Road, Thousand Oaks, CA 91320 (805) 499–5831

Vertical Data Systems, 1215 Meyerside Drive, Unit 2, Mississauga, Ontario, Canada L5T 1H5 (416) 671–1752

Victor Business Products, 3900 N. Rockwell Street, Chicago, IL 60618 (312) 539–8200

Victory Computer Systems, Inc., 2055 Gateway Place, Suite 300, San Jose, CA 95110 (408) 295–4600

Wang Laboratories, Inc., One Industrial Avenue, Lowell, MA 01851 (617) 851–4111

WICAT Systems, 1875 South State Street, Orem, UT 84057 (801) 224–6400

Xerox Corporation, 1341 W. Mockingbird Lane, Dallas TX 75247 (214) 689–6000

Zenith Radio Corporation, Zenith Data Systems Division, 1000 Milwaukee Avenue, Glenview, IL 60025 (312) 391–8860

Zilog, Inc., 1315 Dell Avenue, Campbell, CA 95008 (408) 370–6400

INDEX